Lead

A Collection

Compiled by Swami Jnanamritananda
English translation by Dr. M.N. Namboodiri
from the Malayalam original ***Jyotirgamaya***
by Sri Mata Amritanandamayi

Mata Amritanandamayi Center
San Ramon, CA

LEAD US TO THE LIGHT
A Collection of Mata Amritanandamayi's Teachings
By Sri Mata Amritanandamayi
Malayalam original: *Jyotirgamaya*
Compiled by Swami Jnanamritananda
English translation by Dr. M.N. Namboodiri

ISBN 1-879410-82-6

Published by:
Mata Amritanandamayi Center
P.O. Box 613
San Ramon, CA 94583

asatomā sadgamaya
tamasomā jyotirgamaya
mṛityormā amṛtamgamaya
oṁ śāntiḥ śāntiḥ śāntiḥ

Om, lead us from untruth to truth,
from darkness to light,
and from death to immortality.
Om, peace, peace, peace.

Brihadaranyaka Upanishad (1: 3: 28)

Contents

Foreword

This text is a translation of the Malayalam original, *Jyotirgamaya*, a compilation of Mother's monthly messages in the form of questions and answers, which have appeared in *Matruvani* magazine over the last decade.

Mother's every word spreads the light of knowledge and removes the clouds of confusion that may gather in the minds of Her children. Some conversations are centered on a particular topic. On other occasions, the questions posed address uncertainties that arise in the minds of the listeners. Mother gives appropriate responses to all of them. Her only aim is the spiritual progress of Her children.

Questioning is a sign of growth taking place in the mind. But if doubts are not removed, they will hinder the progress of the individual, and should therefore be cleared immediately. Only then will the journey forward be possible. The words of a *mahatma* (great soul) can be fully trusted to free from confusion those who thirst for spiritual knowledge.

Every word uttered by Mother illumines the path ahead. In the following pages we can read Her answers to the questions and uncertainties that plague the modern age, answers given from the strength of perfect reason and the authority of Her experience.

Swami Jnanamritananda
Amritapuri
24 August, 2000

The Lord of Yoga—Protector of Dharma

Question – The personality of Lord Krishna permeates the entire history of Indian culture. Yet it is hard to explain many of His actions. Some of His actions could even seem unrighteous. What would you say in answer to this?

Mother – For anyone who has really understood the Supreme Being, Sri Krishna, there won't be any doubts regarding His actions. His life will continue to be a model for people of the coming ages, just as it has in ages past. His glory is unsurpassable. His story is a source of joy and inspiration for people from all walks of life.

If a restaurant serves only one type of food, it will attract only those who like that particular cuisine. But if a variety of dishes is offered, all kinds of people will be drawn there; there will be something for everyone. Lord Krishna's teachings are suitable for everyone. He didn't come for a particular section of society. He showed everyone—even prostitutes, robbers, and murderers—the path toward spiritual progress.

The Lord inspires us to follow our *dharma*.[1] His is not a call to act unrighteously or to persist in *adharmic*[2] actions. He urges us to live according to our true dharma, to remain steadfast in it, and thus advance in life toward the ultimate goal.

The Lord doesn't ask us to waste our time, brooding and lamenting over past mistakes. That is not His way. He teaches us to correct our mistakes and move forward. There is no sin that cannot be washed away by the tears of remorse. But once we know what is right, we shouldn't continue repeating what is wrong. The mind should develop the strength necessary to stay on the right course. The Lord showed us how to do this. He taught us the most appropriate way for each one of us. He taught us how to pull ourselves up from whatever level we are on. One person's path may not necessarily be suitable for someone else. This doesn't reflect any shortcomings on the part of the Lord or His teachings; it is simply an accommodation for the differences in people's *samskaras*.[3]

The Supreme Being, Sri Krishna, came to uplift everyone. People question some of His actions only because they do not really try to understand Him. Viewing the landscape from the ground level, we may see hills and valleys, fields and forests. But if we look down on the scene from far above, we will see everything as one expanse of greenery. So, it is really a question of our vantage point. If we survey the Lord's actions from the proper perspective, we can clearly see that His every action was meant to raise

---

1 In Sanskrit dharma means "that which upholds (Creation)." Most commonly it is used to indicate that which is responsible for the harmony of the universe. Dharma has many meanings, including the divine law, the law of existence, righteousness, religion, duty, responsibility, virtue, justice, goodness, and truth. Dharma signifies the inner principles of religion. One well-known definition of dharma is that it leads to the spiritual upliftment and general well-being of all beings in Creation.

2 Adharma is the opposite of dharma.

3 Samskara is the totality of impressions imprinted in the mind by experiences from this or earlier lives, which influence the life of a human being—his or her nature, actions, state of mind, etc. It also means the inherent goodness and refinement of character within each person, and the mental disposition and noble qualities one has cultivated in the past.

people spiritually. However, if we look through eyes tainted with doubts, everything will appear to be wrong. Those who view the world in that way cannot see any good in anyone. This is not God's fault; it is due to a defect of their inner samskara. But Lord Krishna shows even such people the way to upliftment. It is because the Lord's teachings haven't been properly absorbed that India has deteriorated to such an extent.

A child receives a birthday present beautifully wrapped in dazzling colored paper. Fascinated by the wrapping, she doesn't bother to open the packet. She doesn't find the valuable gift inside. This is what has happened to people in regard to Lord Krishna. Some were captivated by the miracles He performed; others saw only mistakes in His deeds and criticized Him. Neither side grasped the real essence. Because of this, they missed the Lord Himself. Both sides discarded the fruit and fought for the peels! They were not ready to grasp the message of His life. Instead of heaping praise or criticism on the mahatmas, we should imbibe the message behind their blessed lives. Thus, we ourselves can lead peaceful, blissful lives, and become role models for the world.

Question – Didn't the Lord stray from the path of truth on many occasions during the Kurukshetra War?

Mother – We cannot really understand or absorb the Lord's deeds with our small minds. His every action, every movement He made, was firmly rooted in dharma. It isn't possible to understand the actions of a mahatma from an ordinary point of view. Only through deep contemplation and purity of heart can we get even an inkling of the meaning of a *mahatma's* deeds.

A mahatma has no ego. He or she is like a bird—the rules of the road do not apply to the birds in the sky. But people who still have a sense of ego have to live by rules.

The Lord always acted in a manner that suited particular circumstances. He had only one goal: to restore dharma. He acknowledged the position of the individual, but when He had to deal with society, it was to society that He gave the greatest importance. Look at the Sri Krishna of the *Bhagavad Gita*. It was not for His own sake that He—who taught about the Supreme Self—participated in the war.

Question – Thousands of people lose their lives during a war. So wasn't Lord Krishna endorsing violence when He urged Arjuna to fight?

Mother – Lord Krishna never wanted war. His way was one of utmost tolerance. But when the tolerance of a powerful person encourages someone to hurt others and to indulge in violence, then that tolerance becomes an even greater violence. If our tolerance makes another person more egoistic, it is best to give it up. But we should be careful not to harbor any feelings of vengeance or resentment toward that person. We shouldn't be against the individual, only against the wrong actions he or she commits.

The Lord felt no hatred toward Duryodhana. He only wanted him to give up his evil ways. This was necessary for the welfare of the people and the country. Only because there was no other way to achieve that goal did the Supreme Being, Sri Krishna, give His consent to the war. He, who was capable of destroying the entire world, made the pledge not to wield any weapons in the war, and to participate only as a charioteer. Doesn't this prove that He had no interest in fighting?

If Duryodhana had offered the Pandavas just one house to live in, Sri Krishna would have pacified the Pandavas and urged them to be content with that. But the Kauravas refused to show even that much compassion.[4] It was the Kauravas, Duryodhana in particular, who compelled others to go to war.

When a country lies in the hands of a ruler who is the very embodiment of unrighteousness, it could cause the destruction of the world. Such people should be removed as soon as possible, by whatever means necessary. That is showing compassion toward society. When you cut down a poisonous tree, some small plants around it may also be destroyed. When you plant a fruit tree, you will perhaps uproot a few small plants to clear a space for the sapling. But think of how beneficial the sapling will be for society after it matures and becomes a tree. And many small plants will flourish in its shade. Viewed in this light, the initial destruction of a few small plants, while regrettable, is an acceptable loss; it isn't violence as such. Had Duryodhana been allowed to live, he would have invaded other kingdoms and killed a greater number of people than died in the Mahabharata War. His actions would also have brought even greater harm to society and civilization in the future. It is far more desirable to protect dharma, even at the cost of a few lives, than to allow adharmic people to rule indefinitely at the cost of many more lives and the

4 Half of the kingdom belonged to the Pandavas. Having returned from 12 years of exile, the Pandavas expected to have their half of the kingdom returned to them; but their cousin Duryodhana refused.

total degeneration of dharma. This is what Sri Krishna did—He protected dharma. War was the only option available if dharma was to survive. What the Lord did was completely appropriate. Had He acted for His own personal benefit, one could perhaps criticize Him; but none of His actions were selfish. He didn't act for His own or His family's sake. The motive behind everything He did was to protect and preserve dharma, to let people live in joy and contentment.

Question – Was it right for the Lord to urge Arjuna to fight?

Mother – The Lord taught us how to live with an understanding of dharma and adharma. He taught that even war is acceptable if there is no other way to uphold dharma. But His way was never one of impulsive action. He demonstrated that one should take up arms only if the enemy refuses to adopt the path of dharma, even after being given ample opportunities to correct his or her errors.

Each individual has his or her own dharma and should be willing to live accordingly; otherwise that person and the whole social order will be affected in a negative way. A mahatma doesn't wish to harm anyone, nor does the mahatma have any special attachment toward anyone. The only desire of the great souls is that dharma be upheld in society. They work toward this goal, in accordance with the prevailing circumstances.

If the room of a house caught on fire, would you advise people to just sit nearby and meditate? No. You would urge them to pour water on the fire and extinguish it as quickly as possible. If necessary, you wouldn't hesitate to cut some plants or tree branches and use them to beat out the fire. That would be the proper thing to do in that situation. This is what Krishna did. A courageous person, having adopted the right course of action after a great deal of thought, would never turn and run away, for to do so goes against dharma.

A mahatma gives more importance to the welfare of society than to the happiness or sadness of any individual. If Duryodhana and his supporters had been allowed to thrive, society would have been riddled with evil. Lord Krishna knew that dharma could be maintained only if those individuals were destroyed. This is why He urged Arjuna to fight. To stand passively by and watch as evil unfolds, without taking any action or feeling any concern, is an even greater evil.

It was Duryodhana who caused the war. Sri Krishna showed him many ways to avoid war, but Duryodhana refused to accept His suggestions.

The Kauravas appropriated whatever they possessed through crooked means. They cheated at the game of dice and took everything the Pandavas owned. The Pandavas, on the other hand, firmly adhered to the principle of truth, without ever abandoning it. The Lord tried to negotiate on their behalf, but the Kauravas would not yield. The Lord explained to the Kauravas that the Pandavas didn't want the whole country; half of it would suffice. The Kauravas refused to agree. In that case, He asked, would they at least give the five Pandavas a house each to live in? No, they said. What about just one house?—the Lord was willing to accept even that. Only when the Kauravas grew so arrogant that they declared they wouldn't give the Pandavas enough land to prick with a needle did Sri Krishna finally accept the inevitability of war. What would have been the consequences for society if those adharmic people had been tolerated? Especially as they were not just ordinary people, but the rulers of the land! If the country had fallen into the hands of such leaders, the result would have been total ruin. Goodness and dharma would have disappeared from the land, resulting in the downfall of the people and the country. It is the dharma of a mahatma to eliminate adharma, to re-establish dharma, and to protect people. To achieve this, Lord Krishna used the Pandavas as His instruments.

Rulers should look upon their subjects as their own kith and kin. But the Kauravas viewed people as their enemies. What good can a country expect from leaders who don't even treat their own cousins justly?

Lord Krishna was infinitely forgiving. He set out to counsel the Kauravas on dharma. But when He arrived at the royal court they attempted to disgrace Him. To allow such people to go free for any reason whatsoever would be to do society and the cause of dharma a great injustice.

The Lord tried all four traditional means—conciliation, charity, reprimand, and punishment. Only after all else failed, did He resort to war in order to destroy the perpetrators of adharma.

There was once a spiritual master who had a disciple in the army. War broke out with another country. The disciple had never fought in a war. Having heard many terrible war stories, he was scared at the very mention of the word "war." He ran away from the army and went to the master. He said to the master that he no longer wanted to do any work and wished to become a sannyasi (monk). The enemy was advancing. The country would be in peril if there were not enough soldiers to fight the war. The master knew that his disciple wanted to become a renunciate only out of fear and not out of any true detachment. He therefore instilled the disciple with courage and sent him back to the battleground. The master didn't do this because he himself had any interest in war; but at that particular time it was the duty of his disciple to fight because he was a soldier. It is never right to be a coward and run away; nor can a person who lacks courage ever attain liberation by taking the vows of a monk. The master taught the disciple about his proper dharma and gave him the strength to carry it out.

Would it be right to tell a soldier on the battlefield to give up everything and become a monk because that is the path to liberation? Soldiers have the responsibility of safeguarding the security of their country. If they fail to carry out their duty, they betray both themselves and the country. When a country's safety is at stake, a soldier's dharma is not to leave the world and become a renunciate, but to fight the enemy. If the soldier at that time decides to renounce everything, he won't succeed—nature won't permit it.

The great spiritual masters are born to make people aware of dharma and to lead the world toward that righteous path. If soldiers don't adhere to their duty, the country will be in peril and the population will suffer. To avoid this, the only advice a true teacher can give a soldier is that he properly perform his duty. This doesn't mean that great masters endorse killing or violence. They simply urge people to follow the path of dharma appropriate at that time period. Thus, we should examine the circumstances when we evaluate the words and deeds of a mahatma.

Arjuna's situation was no different from that of the soldier in the story. He, too, expressed a desire to renounce everything. His wish arose out of his attachment toward his kith and kin on the opposite side of the battlefield. But, at that point, Arjuna's dharma was not to renounce the world, but rather to fight in the war. His desire for renunciation didn't stem from a discerning understanding of the eternal and the fleeting; it came from his attachment. The Lord knew this, and thus He urged Arjuna to fight.

The Lord did not tell Arjuna to go into battle for war's own sake; He urged him to adhere to his dharma. If the Lord had wanted war, He could have persuaded the Pandavas to fight long before, as there was no need to wait. If one strays from one's own dharma out of attachment or fear, or for any other reason, this creates a damaging effect on society and the entire country. The mahatmas know this, and so they urge people to follow the path of dharma appropriate to the circumstances.

Those who know the Self are always compassionate. They wish to see society thrive in peace and harmony, avoiding discord and battles. Only if dharma prevails can this be achieved. This is the model the Supreme Being, Sri Krishna, places before us.

Question – Even though it is said that everyone was equal in Krishna's eyes, didn't He have a special attachment towards the Pandavas?

Mother – Not one action of the Lord stemmed from attachment. Would a person who feels no attachment toward his own kith and kin, including his own children, feel attached to anyone else? Even when Sri Krishna's sons and relatives later fought amongst themselves and perished because of their arrogance, He didn't lose His equipoise. There was no change in the expression of His face. No person with the slightest trace of attachment can illumine the path of dharma for the world. A mind clouded by attachment cannot distinguish between right and wrong.

The Lord didn't show any preference between Duryodhana and Arjuna when they both came to him seeking help before the war. He gave them what they requested. When Duryodhana asked for Sri Krishna's army, the Lord gave it without any hesitation. Arjuna asked for nothing but the Lord Himself. Arjuna didn't waver in his decision even when Sri Krishna explained to him that He would not take up arms during the battle. It was because of Arjuna's selfless devotion and attitude of surrender, not out of any sense of attachment, that the Lord sided with the Pandavas.

One person is offered water, but declines the offer and pushes the cup away. Another person, tormented by thirst, craves water and is given as much as he likes. Can this be called attachment on the part of the giver? Duryodhana didn't want the Lord; he wanted his army. Arjuna had no desire for the Lord's weapons; he wanted only the Lord Himself. Krishna granted both their wishes.

The Lord kept His promise and became Arjuna's charioteer. When, on the battlefield, Arjuna took refuge in the Lord as a disciple, He revealed to Arjuna his dharma through the words of the Bhagavad Gita. Thus, when the underlying power of one's action is free from attachment, knowledge of the Self becomes the guide that shows the way. The Lord showed both Arjuna and Duryodhana His cosmic form. Duryodhana scorned it as some sort of magic. But Arjuna believed—and surrendered himself at the Lord's feet. Arjuna's faith and humility earned the Pandavas their victory.

Only because of Sri Krishna's presence among them were the Pandavas able to forgive the Kauravas for their grave injustice. Had Krishna not been there, the Pandavas would have destroyed Duryodhana long ago. The path of dharma is not one of rashness or arrogance, but one of utmost tolerance and humility. This is what the Lord showed the world through the example of the Pandavas.

Question – Is it right to adopt a path of violence even for the preservation of dharma?

Mother – When judging whether a course of action is violent or nonviolent, we shouldn't just examine the deed itself. It is the attitude behind the deed that is important.

A woman employs a girl to clean the house and gives her a heavier workload than she can handle. However hard the maid tries, she cannot manage. She ends up in tears because of the scolding she receives from her employer. She has no one to console her. The same woman spanks her daughter for wasting time playing instead of doing her homework. Her daughter sits in a corner of the room and cries. Both the girls—the daughter and the employee—are in tears. The spanking given to the daughter cannot be called violence, because the mother punished her with the positive intention of improving her future. This isn't violence, but an expression of love for her daughter.

Though the woman didn't beat the employee, her behavior toward her was cruel. It was, in fact, a form of violence. Would a true mother behave like that toward her own child? Here, we should pay attention to the different attitudes behind these two actions.

A patient suffering from a fatal disease dies during an operation. Yet everyone praises the doctor for his enormous effort to save the patient's life. Elsewhere, a thief with the same type of knife used by the doctor during the operation stabs a watchman who tries to prevent him from stealing. While the doctor's action was nonviolent (*ahimsa*), the robber's act was violent (*himsa*).

When there is more than enough food for a meal, it would be a form of violence to kill a chicken just to make an extra dish to improve the enjoyment of the dinner. To pick a flower that we do not need is also an act of violence.

It is the attitude behind an action that makes it either violent or nonviolent. The harm done to any living being out of selfishness, to enhance our own happiness or comfort, is a form of violence. But if we must inflict pain on a harmful individual for the welfare of society, this cannot be considered violence. This is why the Mahabharata War is called the War of Dharma.

Question – Sri Krishna killed Kamsa, His own uncle. How can that be justified?

Mother – When we read sacred books such as the *Puranas*, we shouldn't simply accept the stories at face value. We should go deeper than the surface and try to understand the underlying principles. Using stories is like using one's fingers to teach a blind child to read Braille. Stories provide only an aid to grasp principles. Interwoven with each of these stories is the atma tattva (principle of the Self). Only when we discern that deeper principle will we reap the full benefit of the stories.

Sri Krishna aimed to make each person fit for everlasting bliss, for Self-realization. But that state can only be reached through the path of dharma. Some people who lack discrimination feel averse even to the word dharma. Kamsa was one such individual. However much council he was offered, he lacked the mental maturity to accept anyone's advice. Those who forsake the path of dharma can never attain knowledge of the Self.

Lord Krishna came to earth for the sake of both the virtuous and the sinners. His mission also included leading sinners to God. He did everything to instill a sense of dharma in those on the wrong path. But they were drunk with the notion of the body as the self, and refused to embrace dharma. Only one option remained open to the Lord: to destroy their bodies, which were the inspiration of all their evil acts and supported all of their externally driven senses. So he allowed this to happen. It was the only way to convince them of the impermanence of the body and the eternal nature of the Self. Only through that experience could they gain the understanding that they were the heirs to eternal bliss, which lies beyond the reach of the senses.

Sometimes a mother discards her baby's clothes because the clothes are too dirty to wash. She does this only to clothe her baby in new garments. Would you call that an injustice? In the case of an adharmic person who is threatening the lives of others and the welfare of society, when all other means fail, the last resort may be to liberate that person from his or her existing body. When that soul attains a new body, it may realize the greatness of dharma and proceed along the right path toward the ultimate goal. When a plantain tree is infested with an incurable, untreatable disease, it is cut down close to its base. This prevents the new shoots from being infected. The new plants will grow to be healthy and yield good fruits.

The Lord knew that Kamsa would never adhere to the path of dharma in that lifetime. His mind and body were completely steeped in adharma. That body had to go and a new one had to be acquired. When he died at the hands of the Lord, he left his body with his eyes gazing at Krishna, and with his mind focused on Him. Thus all his sins were washed away. It was, in fact, Kamsa's innermost desire to die at the hands of the Lord. And the Lord fulfilled that desire.

But even though outwardly Sri Krishna killed Kamsa, what actually happened is not that apparent. The Lord lifted Kamsa's soul out of his body and created the right circumstances for Kamsa to reach the Supreme Self. He destroyed Kamsa's ego and lifted his soul to the supreme state.

Suppose you have drawn lions and leopards on a wall. If you erase those drawings, the animals no longer exist—just a clear wall remains. The wall served as the foundation of those animal forms. If we want, we can also draw deer or rabbits on the same wall. So, did the death of the lions and the leopards really take place? Were deer and rabbits ever really born? In reality, only a few lines on the wall changed and thus their names and forms changed with them. The underlying wall always remains. Similarly, the Lord only destroyed the egoistic nature in Kamsa. He didn't destroy the Self within him. We should understand this.

Question – Aren't some of Krishna's deeds, for example, the theft of the gopis' clothes and the rasa-lila, unbecoming for a divine incarnation?

Mother – Those who criticize the Lord for stealing those clothes can only be called ignorant, because Sri Krishna was only six or seven years old at that time. His aim was to make everyone happy. He wanted to break the artificial limitations of pride and shame, and to awaken each soul to the Supreme Being. A baby straddling his mother's hip doesn't think about his clothes. Each of us should develop the attitude of being God's tender baby. We should cultivate the attitude of total innocence, untouched by body-consciousness, toward God. God cannot be attained without giving up the sense of pride and shame. Without letting go of our body-consciousness, we cannot rise to the level of the Self.

In olden days, the women of Kerala generally didn't cover their breasts. People didn't find this strange at all. But how would people react today? Similarly, the way people in western countries dress during the summer would appear objectionable to us in India. But as it is the prevailing custom in the West and people are used to it, they find nothing wrong with it. Even those Indians who presently feel disturbed by it would change their attitude if they stayed in the West for any length of time. Some of them may even adopt that way of dressing.

Feelings of pride and shame are creations of the mind. Only by breaking those chains that tightly bind the mind can we reach the feet of God.

Mother[5] doesn't mean that everyone should give up wearing clothes! She means only that nothing should stand in the way of our unbroken remembrance of God. What we need is freedom from all bonds that draw our minds away from God.

The *rasa-lila* did not take place on the ordinary plane of the senses, the way people today interpret it. During the rasa-lila the *gopis* experienced the beatitude of merging the individual soul with the Supreme Being. Because of their divine love, the Lord appeared to each of the gopis. With His power, He blessed each gopi with a vision of the Self.

The rasa-lila is something that a mind reveling in the senses cannot even imagine. Only when the mind and the senses are freed from all attachments to sense objects can one hope to experience even the smallest fraction of the divine bliss that the gopis enjoyed during the rasa-lila.

Each gopi, in her relationship with Lord Krishna, had the attitude of the lover toward the Beloved (*madhura bhava*). This attitude also exists in Christianity. Nuns consider themselves to be brides of Lord Jesus. Does this taint Christ in any way? It represents the relationship between the individual soul and the Supreme Being. Only those who observe everything through worldly eyes could find fault with this.

The Lord wasted no opportunity to lead people of all kinds to eternal bliss. Through every possible situation,

5 Mother often refers to Herself in the third person.

He attempted to brighten the flame of the Self within people and to add the fuel of His love to the light of the Self shining in their hearts. The Lord is responsible for Creation and is also the One who liberates the soul from Creation. Liberation is possible only through the removal of body-consciousness. Here lies the very objective of His incarnation as Krishna.

Question – In the Gita, Lord Krishna says that whatever happens, we should never abandon our own dharma. If that is so, how can a person leave his or her profession for another job that is more profitable?

Mother – In those days, many people believed that they could attain liberation only by giving up all karma (work), retreating into the forest and living as sannyasis. In response, the Lord proclaimed that it isn't necessary to forsake everything, but that people should perform their duties in the world, firmly established in their own dharma. The Lord made it clear that we shouldn't abandon our duties, but rather that performing those duties with the right attitude leads us to liberation.

There exists another dimension to this concept of dharma. A child born into the family of a sculptor can easily become a good sculptor, because the circumstances favor that potential. Most likely, the child was born with the same gift. The father's or mother's talent passes to the child as the child's heritage. It may take such a child ten days to grasp what others would take a year to learn. Thus, there lies great potential to advance if one works steadfastly in one's hereditary craft. Others coming from outside the craft will have to learn it starting from scratch.

At that time, people performed their traditional vocations mostly in their own homes. They didn't work in an office or in a factory. Everyone in the family joined in the traditional work. People used to enter their family profession after receiving their education at a gurukula. To which of the four main castes[6] one belonged was decided on the basis of the profession one chose, and not on one's birth. No one is born with a particular caste or religion—all are simply God's children. Only when people grew up were they divided into different castes on the basis of their work. In those days, a child born into the Kshatriya (warrior) caste had the right to become a Brahmin (priest or Vedic teacher), and a child of a Brahmin family could become a Kshatriya. A person who worked with wood was called a carpenter. Even if the carpenter had been born and raised as a Brahmin, he would still be known as a carpenter. It was with the degeneration of the rules of Sanatana Dharma (the Eternal Religion, as Hinduism is called) that a person's birth became the sole basis for his or her caste.

In the olden days, people didn't work just to earn an income. Everyone's goal in life was Self-realization, and one's work was a means to attain that state. In the perfection of their work, people tasted the experience of God.

When everyone seeks to work only for financial gain, the harmony of the social order will be lost—selfishness and greed will prevail.

In those days, the custom of paying a predetermined wage to workers didn't exist. Workers were paid the amount they needed, and they were satisfied with what they re-

6 The four main castes: Brahmins (priests and Vedic teachers), Kshatriyas (warriors), Vaishyas (merchants), and Sudras (workers).

ceived. An atmosphere of love existed between workers and their employers. They respected one another. Those who paid wages and those who received them were both fully satisfied. That custom disappeared when people grew more selfish. The attitude of employers changed to "Less pay, more work," and employees began to think, "Less work, more pay."

It is said that when you visit a temple, you shouldn't count the money you offer the deity; you should give by the handfuls. These days, people put aside small change, so that even if they give a whole handful, it won't amount to more than a few rupees.

Today most people want their children to become engineers and doctors, in order to be respected in society and earn a lot of money. Few parents pay any attention to their child's real aptitude. If the spirit of competition that prevails in education is a healthy one, it will help children to advance and bring out their talents. Instead, the competition today causes tension among students. They lose their mental strength when they fail to achieve their aims, and end up spending the rest of their lives in despair. And their despair drives many of them to suicide. This shouldn't be allowed to happen. The aims of education and of securing a job should be our spiritual development and service to the world. These goals will motivate us to advance in any field. Even if we happen to fail, it will only prompt us to try again and not to succumb to despair and waste our lives.

When we select a field as our life's work, we should try to gain as much expertise as possible in that area. We should stick to it and find success in life. The aim of life is not to become a millionaire, but to enjoy eternal bliss. But still, a householder (a person who lives a married life) has a duty to support the family. When accepting remuneration for our work, our only aim should be to earn what we need.

In the old days, people would work hard, keep as much of their wages as they required for themselves and their families, and give the rest to the poor. Today business management is one of the most coveted professions in society. Commerce is necessary for the economic progress of a country, but personal gain shouldn't be the only goal in business; the progress of the country should also be taken into account. Yet, we find many merchants and industrialists who amass not only enough wealth for themselves but for a thousand future generations! At the same time, all around them countless impoverished people struggle, unable to scrape together enough money for even one meal. Hardly anyone thinks about this. The goal of most people today is to make as much profit as possible for themselves, even at the expense of others.

If you leave your field of work and select another, it means that you are not satisfied with your work. But you won't necessarily find contentment in your new ventures either, because contentment depends on the mind and not on external actions or situations. If people leave their professions with a desire to earn excessive profits, it simply shows their greed. Without changing their attitudes, such people will never find contentment in life. But for those who have controlled their minds, every situation will be favorable. They will enjoy any field of work. Nothing will make them feel dissatisfied. We should cultivate this frame of mind in whatever work we do.

If we give up one type of work and start another, we

may temporarily feel satisfied, but it won't necessarily last. A snake lying frozen in the snow will look harmless. But give it a little warmth and it will soon show its true nature, hissing and striking at you. Similarly, the mind will show its true nature as soon as the circumstances arise, and you will lose your peace of mind. The way to control the mind lies not in pampering it and giving it everything it demands. We should control it and turn it toward the real goal. Likewise, the Lord advised Arjuna to stand firm in his duty and thus succeed in life. You may do whatever work you enjoy, but it is your attitude that has to be transformed. Then, even fighting on the battlefield becomes a sacred offering (*yajna*). That was what Sri Krishna counseled. He didn't encourage giving up our work for any selfish reason; nor did He advise opening our third eye while closing the other two. His example teaches us to see through our third eye while keeping the other two eyes open. In other words, Sri Krishna teaches us to face life while beholding the underlying unity in everything.

Question – Even though Sri Krishna had vowed not to take up weapons during the battle, He actually did. Wasn't that wrong?

Mother – Every word and deed of Sri Krishna was for the sake of others, not for Himself. How could He use His weapons when Arjuna and Bhishma, who were both devoted to Him, fought on opposite sides? Thus, He refused to fight. When Bhishma sent thousands of arrows in His direction, He just smiled. When those piercing arrows covered His body with bleeding wounds, He received them like flower petals offered in worship. Bhishma, a devotee, a great warrior, and a man who spoke only the truth, had vowed to force the Lord to use His weapon. Unable to make Sri Krishna waver in His decision, Bhishma began shooting arrows at Arjuna, who was standing just behind the Lord. Now, Arjuna was vulnerable and unable to defend himself against the onslaught of arrows. His chariot began to crumble. He was in grave danger. Without wasting a moment, the Lord leaped down and sprang toward Bhishma with the *sudarshana chakra* (divine discus) in His hand. Thus in one stroke—even though He had to forsake His own pledge—the Lord fulfilled Bhishma's vow only for the sake of protecting Arjuna. Through this act, He satisfied both of His devotees. Because Arjuna was His devotee, He was responsible for protecting Arjuna's life. Because Bhishma was also His devotee, His duty was to make Bhishma's words come true and thus protect Bhishma's honor. For this purpose, He was willing to sacrifice His own reputation as the embodiment of truthfulness. This shows His incomparable compassion.

The flow of God's grace toward the devotee depends not on dharma or on adharma, nor is it governed by the laws of cause and effect. God's grace isn't limited by any rules. This is why the sages praise God as the Ocean of causeless (spontaneous, unmotivated) compassion.

Question – What is the relevance of Rama and Krishna in this scientific age?

Mother – Everyone is enthusiastically extolling the achievements of science. It is true that scientific advances have greatly contributed to the progress of humanity. They have helped increase our material comforts and sense of well-being. Traveling from one place to another is much easier today than in the past. A journey that used to take several days can now be completed in a few minutes. The time saved can be utilized for other purposes. One person using computers can now perform certain tasks which once took a hundred people to complete. It is true that we have made great progress on the material level. But at the same time, people's minds have become weaker. How many people who fully enjoy technological advances are able to sleep peacefully at night? Mother has met countless people who live in air-conditioned rooms, and yet who cannot sleep without sleeping pills. Doesn't this prove that scientific advances alone cannot give you peace of mind? Look at how many millionaires commit suicide. Do they lack anything from a material point of view? Surely, if they had peace of mind, they wouldn't commit suicide. These days many people have everything on the material level, but they don't have what they really need—peace and happiness.

In olden times people didn't have sleeping problems even though there were no such luxuries as air-conditioning. Today those who are used to fans and air-conditioners cannot do without them. If the electricity goes off one night so that those devices do not work, people won't get any sleep. The cells of those who spend all their time in air-conditioned rooms, without breathing any fresh air, are gradually damaged by that atmosphere. It also destroys the natural powers of the body. Some people have to drink tea in the morning, otherwise they'll get a headache. We have developed many bad habits. The mind is the sole cause of this. Our minds and bodies, which once were strong because we lived in harmony with nature, have become weak. Long ago, people lived in perfect harmony with nature. They were not disturbed by climatic changes or by any other changes in nature. But these days people isolate themselves from their natural surroundings; they live in separate, artificial, self-centered worlds. They do not realize that their constant search for temporary pleasures causes them to sink into endless sorrow.

Our ancestors experienced much greater contentment and happiness in life. They were healthier and lived longer than people do today. Huge, magnificent stone structures, including temple towers, stand to this day, as proof of the physical strength of the people of old. Are people today strong enough to lift even one of those stones? There weren't many machines in those days and people knew how to live in harmony with nature.

Science, which is meant to increase the material comforts of people and help them, is instead turning into the death knell of humanity. In the hands of selfish people, technology is used to exploit their fellow beings. Instead of peace and love, competition and violence are thriving in the world. For the achievements of science to benefit everyone, people need to learn how to love, to be compassionate, and to cultivate noble qualities.

Today, every scientific discovery increases the arrogance of people. "Who are you to argue with us? Look at the achievements of our country!" This has become the attitude of every ruler. Day by day, more conflicts grow between individuals and nations. People seem increasingly eager to move away from the shores of love toward the rough waters of arrogance.

Mother is not in any way criticizing or belittling scientific discoveries, but they shouldn't dry up the wellspring of love within us. We have improved the external world, but the inner world is withering away. In the past, people received the training they needed to keep their minds under control in all circumstances. They didn't have to go through life weakened by insignificant things. If you fall into deep water, you won't survive if you don't know how to swim, regardless of what else you may have learned. Likewise, however much you increase your material comforts, you cannot enjoy peace of mind without having trained your mind.

In the future, people will become very weak if they are unable to find repose within themselves, because increasingly there won't be anyone who loves them selflessly. Courageous are those who find peace within their own minds under all circumstances, not those who depend on other people or material objects for happiness. This is what Sri Rama, Sri Krishna, and other divine incarnations teach us.

As a prince, Lord Rama was the darling of His parents, His teachers, and the people of His country. He was living in the midst of regal splendor, when suddenly one morning He was sent into exile in the forest, forced to leave everything behind. The comforts of the palace were no longer available. There was no delicious food, no silken bed to sleep on, no attendants to fan Him. Yet He lived in the forest with the same peace of mind as He'd had in the palace. In His mind, which was in perfect harmony with nature, His kingdom and the forest were the same. Lord Rama found no difficulty in adapting to circumstances as they changed, because His mind was fully under His control. Being an atmarama (one who delights in the Self), He found bliss within Himself alone.

This same quality can also be observed in the lives of the Pandavas. They lived in accordance with Sri Krishna's advice. Not once did they quarrel among themselves. Not even the most difficult tests in life could break their unity or mutual love.

Today when three people live under a single roof, they behave as if they were living on three different planets; there is no real bond between them, no oneness of heart. This is how powerful people's selfishness has grown. If our minds are not strong enough under those circumstances, the rate of mental disease and suicide will increase.

There was a time when a thread of love bound people to one another. Today, people stick to each other with the brittle glue of selfishness, which can crack at any moment, leaving nothing to hold people together.

We are immersed in a culture that encourages impure thoughts and emotions. People's only concern is how to satisfy their senses. All their efforts are aimed toward that end and for this they need a lot of money. To acquire that money, people often resort to corruption, resulting in an increase in crime and violence. In this world of momentary sense gratification, little place remains for a sense of kinship or motherly love, and thus unrest spreads throughout society. It places the security of each country at risk and also destroys the harmony of nature.

In an age such as this, the relevance of the life and teachings of Lord Krishna is greater than ever. What do we learn by studying His teachings? We understand that sense enjoyment and self-gratification can never make us happy, and that true everlasting bliss is found only within ourselves. He teaches us this again and again. However, He doesn't completely negate sensory pleasures. He simply reminds us that there is another meaning and purpose to life.

All excesses should be avoided. We should eat only to satisfy our hunger. Health experts suggest that to maintain good health, no more than half the stomach should be filled with food, one quarter with water, and the remaining quarter left empty. Spiritual science also explains how to maintain our mental health. The idea is not that we shouldn't partake of any sense enjoyments, but that we should never become slaves of our senses or of the habits of the mind. We should be the masters of our mind and senses. Along with enjoyment, it is important to also practice some degree of renunciation. Chocolate is sweet, but too much of it will make us sick. So, we should practice restraint even if we feel like overindulging. There is a limit to the use of everything, and this is for our own good. Self-restraint never hinders freedom. What would happen if people drove as they pleased on the roads, claiming that traffic rules violated their freedom! Traffic rules are essential for everyone's safety. Similarly, observing certain spiritual rules is required if we want to enjoy lasting happiness and contentment.

Viewing the situation from all angles, we can clearly see that putting spiritual principles to work in our daily life is the only way to bring about fundamental changes in today's world. Our intellects have expanded, but our hearts are drying up. Lord Krishna's life gives us an ideal example to follow in order to escape our present condition, to soothe our burning hearts and minds, and to mend the broken thread of love.

Lord Krishna embraces both the spiritual and the material aspects of life. He doesn't ask us to forego one for the sake of the other. When it is time for a plant to bear fruit, the flower petals drop by themselves. Similarly, as our awareness of the goal grows stronger, our attachments to material pleasures drop away naturally. Giving up pleasures is not as important as cultivating the right attitude toward those pleasures. Only when the spiritual and material aspects of life are in balance, like the two wings of a bird, can there be harmony in society.

Lord Krishna gave specific instructions to different types of people from all walks of life—to sannyasis, brahmacharis, householders, soldiers, kings, and the very worldly. He taught the world how each individual can attain realization regardless of his or her background or living conditions. This is why He is called a *Purnavatar*, a complete incarnation of the Divine. He didn't come for the benefit of *sannyasis* only. His life was a perfect example of how to remain unscorched in the midst of worldly fire. It is like keeping a piece of chocolate on your tongue without salivating.

Running away from the responsibilities of life, retiring to the forest, and sitting with our eyes closed isn't that hard. There are few adversaries in the forest that can create difficulties. The Lord doesn't teach us to run away from this world full of suffering. He shows how to succeed in life while remaining in the midst of obstacles. The Lord doesn't advise us to turn away from our relationships in order to attain Self-realization. He explains that we should be free from all attachment while still maintaining loving relationships and upholding our family responsibilities.

Spiritual science teaches us how to face every situation with a smile. A real *yogi* maintains his or her peace of mind in the midst of any crisis. Those who wish to achieve this state need only observe Lord Krishna's life, the perfect model.

The flame of a lantern burns steadily within a glass chimney, protected from the wind. There is nothing commendable in that. A real spiritual person, however, should be like an open flame, bright as the sun, burning steadily even through a raging storm. Lord Krishna should be our role model if we wish to attain that state. He shows us the way to harmonize the two aspects of the mind—the spiritual and the material—and to progress toward perfection.

The liberation the Lord promises is not something to be attained after death; it is attainable here in this world, while still in the body. Throughout His life, Lord Krishna had to face different crises that arose like waves, one after the other. Even then, not once was His countenance clouded by sorrow. He faced every difficult situation with a smile.

For the Supreme Being, Sri Krishna, life was a captivating song of joy from beginning to end. Even the most grief-stricken person felt blissful in His presence. Just as darkness has no place in the sun, there was no place for sorrow in Sri Krishna's presence. He was the embodiment of bliss. In His company, everyone rejoiced, forgetting all else. In His presence they tasted the bliss of the Self. Even now, after all this time, doesn't the mere thought of Him fill us with bliss?

People find fault with the Lord's divine play because their minds remain attached to the senses. Our attempts to measure the infinite glory of the Lord with our relatively puny minds is like the frog in the well trying to measure the ocean.

If we can give up our doubting, critical way of looking at things, and instead with openness and love observe Sri Krishna's life—a life sweet from beginning to end—we will discover that nothing in His life is to be dismissed, that every moment is to be embraced. Only when the inner eye of divine love opens up can we enjoy complete success and perfect peace in this life and hereafter.

Women and Society

Question – What should be the role and status of women in society?

Mother – Women should have the same status as men and an equal share in running society. When the position of women diminishes, society loses its harmony. Men and women have an equal place in God's Creation. Just as one half of the body is as indispensable as the other, men and women have the same importance. One half cannot claim to be superior to the other. When it is said that woman is the left side of man, it goes without saying that man is the right side of woman. The difference between men and women is mainly at the body level.

Just like men, women have their own unique role in society. Each person should understand his or her role and act accordingly. When women try to seize the role of men, or when men control the role of women by force, it causes discontentment and lack of peace in individuals and thereby in society.

The left and right tires of a car are equally important. Only if the wheels on both sides move forward simultaneously can the travelers reach their goal. Similarly, in family life, only when the husband and wife live together in harmony, will they be able to reach the real goal, to unite with the Self.

Women were given a highly respected position in the ancient culture of India. Matrudevo bhava (Be one who looks upon the mother (women) as divine) was the ideal India gave to the world. Our culture teaches men to view all women as their mother. Every man spends nine months in his mother's womb before being born. Naturally, then, a sensible man will view his own mother with respect. All women should be treated with that same respect.

The woman forms the foundation of the family. She can play a greater role than the man in maintaining the peace, harmony, and prosperity of the family, because as a woman she is especially gifted with love, forgiveness, and humility. These qualities in women hold the family together. Masculinity stands for firm willpower. But willpower alone is not enough to maintain a harmonious relationship among family members. Everyone in the family should cultivate love, patience, humility, and a forgiving attitude toward the other family members. Internal conflicts arise in the family when the woman tries to adopt a masculine nature, or when the man attempts to force his ego on the woman.

India is the land of renunciation, not of sensory indulgence. Our ancestors sought and found the fountain of eternal bliss. They did not fall prey to the modern error of wasting life and health in pursuit of fleeting pleasures. A person's position in society was determined by his or her actions, qualities, and dharma. Everyone's ultimate goal was Self-realization. People were fully aware of that goal and the path leading there. This brought contentment. But, then, those who were not contented tried to seize the positions held by others. When there is inner dissatisfaction, conflict is born. The social order in India was fully capable of leading everyone to perfect happiness and

Self-realization. Equality between men and women and the position of women in society were not issues of debate in those days.

A woman's true place in society is by no means in the back row. It is equal to that of men—she belongs in the front row. The important question is whether or not she is given that position today.

Question – Doesn't Manu[7] say that a woman's father should protect her in childhood, her husband in her youth, and her sons in her old age, and that a woman is not fit for independence?

Mother – The true meaning of this is that a woman deserves to be protected, not that she should be denied freedom. Manu points out that it is the responsibility of men to protect women under all circumstances. This shows that women held a high position in society. A woman shouldn't have to be given freedom by anyone; to enjoy as much freedom as any man is her birthright. But Manu says it is the duty of men to ensure her protection. A society that denies women their freedom is courting its own destruction.

When Mother hears people criticize this statement by Manu, She is reminded of the police protection given to ministers when they travel. Are the ministers not free because they are being protected? They enjoy full freedom and can travel anywhere. It is simply the duty of the policemen around them to ensure that freedom. In the same way, our society, which gave full freedom to women, made it the responsibility of men to ensure the women's protec-

7 See Glossary.

tion and safety. Indian society bestowed this honorable position on women because women act as the guiding lights of the family, and thus, ultimately, of the entire society.

Question – What is Mother's opinion about the debate on the equality between men and women?

Mother – We should be talking about the unity of men and women, and not so much about their equality. It is difficult for men and women to achieve equality at the body level. If you observe the mental plane, there is a certain amount of masculinity in women and an element of femininity in men. Women shouldn't blindly imitate men. If, for example, they try to imitate men by indulging in gambling, drinking, and smoking, they are digging the grave of womanhood. Instead, they need to nurture the masculine element within themselves. And men should cultivate the motherly aspect within themselves. This is perfection. Through the inner enhancement of these opposites in both men and women, both will move toward wholeness and perfection.

Materialistic cultures consider the relationship between a man and a woman to be confined mostly to the physical plane, but the culture of India has taught us to view it as a bond on the spiritual plane.

These days, what many people desire in the name of freedom for married women is really only freedom from the responsibilities of family life. Unlimited freedom, without any responsibilities, will only foster a desire for material enjoyment. How can peace and harmony be maintained in a family where there is a spirit of competition between the partners? At the same time, when a man and a woman move forward together with love, mutual understanding, and a willingness to be flexible to the other's needs, what develops is not equality between them, but union—the union of Shiva and Shakti. That is the world of joy. The man and the woman become one, forgetting all differences. Each one makes up for the deficiencies of the other. Through love, each transcends any anger in the other; and through forbearance, each accepts the weaknesses of the other. In this way, both enjoy real freedom. People need this blending of the masculine and feminine qualities in life. The feminine power complements the man, while the masculine power complements the woman. In a relationship, each needs support, encouragement, and inspiration from the other. They are not a burden to each other, but are supportive and protective. To achieve this ideal, we need to understand spirituality. Spirituality helps us to forget external conflicts and to realize our inner union, the essence of the Self.

Question – It is said that women were denied social equality in India. Weren't Indian women condemned to confinement in the chambers of the home?

Mother – The history of India differs from that of other countries in many ways. Indian civilization is older than any other civilization. Women once held a place of honor in our society. Even during Vedic sacrifices, men and women had equal rights in performing sacrifices, and when a man performed the Vedic sacrifices, he and his wife shared equal status. Women even contributed several Vedic mantras. In ancient times, a woman had the same right as a man to choose any profession. Women such as Maitreyi and Gargi held venerable places in the assembly of scholars. In those days, India also had women warriors. If we study the counsel given in the Ramayana by women such as Sumitra, Tara, and Mandodari, we will see that in the matter of dharma women stood as a decisive force. How can it be said that women were denied freedom in such a civilization?

It is true that India has been influenced from time to time by the cultural changes in foreign countries. We can see this by carefully studying India's history. For centuries, India was forced to exist under foreign rule. The foreigners ruling India looked upon women as no more than objects of enjoyment. To escape those people, women often had to remain confined to their homes. Gradually, elements of decay crept into our culture as well. This caused much destruction to the great civilization that once flourished in India.

While traditionally India embraced the joy and deathlessness of renunciation, the rulers who occupied the land considered sense enjoyment and indulgence as their goal in life. How could there be harmony between people of such different mindsets? India's system of education also changed with the arrival of Westerners. Gurukula education vanished. The purpose of education changed from the development of self-reliance to the development of dependence on others. Teachings about dharma, such as *Matru devo bhava, pitru devo bhava, acharya devo bhava* (Treat your mother as divine; treat your father as divine; treat your teacher as divine), were no longer taught in schools. Selfishness and competition replaced truth and renunciation. Women who originally had sought refuge from the foreign conquerors in the inner chambers of their homes were now compelled to remain there by the new generations of men whose predominant characteristic was selfishness. These new generations distorted the ethical codes and scriptural rules to suit their own selfish interests. Society bears the consequence of this even now. The basic reason for the choking experience women have had to undergo in India comes from the influence of other cultures. Forcing a woman to suffer doesn't belong to Indian culture; that stems from another, *rakshasic* (demonic) culture. We should remember that Sita's tears reduced Lanka to ashes.[8]

Question – When Mother says that completeness is attained through the unity of the masculine and the feminine, does Mother mean that completeness cannot be achieved through *brahmacharya*?

Mother – By the merging of man and woman, Mother doesn't mean on the physical level. What makes someone a woman or a man is the predominant feminine or masculine element in that person. Women and men contain both elements. Regarding a woman in whom a masculine nature is dominant, we say that even though she is a woman, she is like a man. Similarly, we look at a man in whom femininity is dominant, and say that he is like a woman. We don't say this on the basis of their bodies, of course.

The woman is unaware of the masculinity within her and searches for it on the outside, in a man. Likewise, the man doesn't try to nourish the qualities of forgiveness,

8 This refers to the ancient epic, the Ramayana, written by Sage Valmiki. Sita was the wife of the divine Incarnation Lord Rama. After they had been sent into exile in the forest, Sita was kidnapped by the demon Ravana and taken to Lanka. Rama sent his helpers to search for her. Rama's great devotee, the monkey god, Hanuman, found her in Lanka. After seeing Sita, Hanuman burned part of the city to ashes. At the end of the epic, Ravana is killed by Lord Rama and Sita is rescued.

compassion, and affection that lie hidden within him. He imagines they are to be found only in a woman. Both men and women should awaken the complementary powers and capacities within themselves. Completeness is the union of the masculine and feminine elements within ourselves. That is what the *ardhanarisvara* image symbolizes. Only through this inner union can we experience limitless bliss.

The aim of brahmacharya is to realize that both the male and female aspects are contained within us, and that the nature of our true Self transcends any such duality. We cannot experience this without constant spiritual practice. But people today don't have the patience for that. They consider everything they see in the external world to be real, and run after the mirage of sense pleasures, perishing in that pursuit.

Question – What are Mother's views on women seeking advanced educational qualifications?

Mother – Women should attain the same high level of education as men, and they should find work if necessary. Proper education is the wellspring of social justice and a noble culture.

Only if a woman attains self-reliance through education can she encourage, inspire, and counsel her partner in life as a true *sahadharmini*—the wife who takes every step in life at her husband's side on the path of dharma.

Also, the main reason that women are forced to suffer in the family and in society today is their lack of financial freedom. If they can secure jobs that provide them with an income, their financial bondage will be eliminated. Because of the influence of our present culture and a general ignorance about spiritual matters, people have a completely materialistic view of life. They give far greater importance to worldly matters such as financial wealth than to the spiritual unity of the masculine and feminine. This change in attitude is one of the reasons for the increasing number of divorces. Women should lay the foundation for their financial independence and security today; otherwise, under the present circumstances, as long as a woman is undereducated and not financially self-reliant, she will not be able to support herself tomorrow when the need arises.

Family ties are not very strong in the West. In due course, the western habit of men leaving their wives for other women will cease to be considered wrong in India as well. Apart from taking care of their own needs, women will also have to shoulder most of the responsibilities of raising their children. They will suffer a lot of hardships if they don't find a source of steady income beforehand. But they cannot do this without a higher education.

Question – But we don't see that women attempted to receive a high education in the old days.

Mother – The circumstances are totally different now from what they were then. The needs of life were simple in those days. There was no need for both husband and wife to earn money. Furthermore, the purpose of education was not merely to earn money; it was to make a person fit to reach the supreme state, through the awakening of his or her true Self. Women acquired this knowledge during childhood. The bride became the woman of the house and was regarded as the source of all the wealth and prosperity of her husband and the family. Only the husband worked to earn the resources necessary to meet the family's expenses. In this environment, the wife didn't feel that her husband curtailed her freedom and made her his slave, and the husband didn't feel that his wife was the ruler of the family. Love, not selfishness, bound them together. A woman in those days saw it as her duty, her dharma, to manage the family, to serve her husband and his parents, and to take care of the children. The husband, in turn, felt that his own happiness lay in his wife's security and well-being. There is no place for conflict in such a family; it is a family filled with peace. Our peace comes from the noble qualities we live by. Wealth, position, and status cannot bring us peace. In those days women didn't feel the need to get a higher education or to secure a job to bring in more income.

Question – These days, when both parents work, how can they give their children the attention they need?

Mother – As long as they understand how important it is to do so, they will surely find time for their children. No matter how busy people are in their work, they still manage to take time off when they get sick, don't they?

Women have to be careful from the beginning of their pregnancies. A pregnant woman should avoid any situations that may create tension, because stress experienced during pregnancy could cause health problems in the infant she carries. This is why a pregnant woman should try to be happy, do spiritual practice, visit ashrams, and seek advice from spiritual masters.

Mothers should understand how important it is to breastfeed their babies. Breast milk is the milk of love; it is formed out of the love of the mother for her baby. It also contains many easily digested nutrients. It is ideal for the baby's health and for strengthening the baby's memory power. Nothing equals breast milk.

When the child is old enough to remember things, the parents should begin imparting moral lessons to the child through stories and lullabies. In the past, the household usually included grandparents and other relatives as well. Today people usually consider their aging parents a burden. They move out and set up separate households as soon as possible. In the process, their own children are deprived of the rich, fertile soil of family relationships. The children also miss out on the numerous little stories that grandpa and grandma could tell. The children become stunted in their development, like a sapling planted in a pot, unable to grow deep roots or develop to its full potential. In today's world, it would be best to entrust the responsibility of the children to the elders in the family. They will care for their grandchildren with more love and affection than any nanny or day-care worker could provide. The presence of the children will also add joy to the lives of the grandparents in their old age.

It is from the mother's lap that children learn their first lessons on how to distinguish between right and wrong. Their personalities are molded by the influences they imbibe until the age of five. During this time, children normally spend most of their time with their parents. These days, as day-care centers have become popular, children miss out to a large extent on their mother's selfless love and affection. The caretakers at day-care centers are paid employees. Many of them have their own children at home to love and cherish. A mother won't feel the same emotional bond with someone else's child as she feels with her own. Thus, at the very time when the children's characters need to be molded, their minds become closed. How can such children later be expected to feel a sense of responsibility to care for their elderly parents, the same parents who once entrusted them to day-care workers at the tender age when they needed to develop in the warmth of their mother's love? It would be surprising if those children didn't think of putting their elderly parents in nursing homes.

The mother is the one who guides the child. Apart from providing love and affection to the child she bears and nurtures, she also has the responsibility of helping the child to develop noble qualities. She can do this ten times more effectively than the father. Hence the saying that when a man is good, it benefits one individual, but when a woman is good, it benefits the whole family.

In children who grow up without receiving enough love, an animal nature often dominates rather than a kind heart. This is unavoidable if the parents don't have any spiritual values. Parents should make a distinction between more trivial needs and the absolute necessities of life. They should find satisfaction in a simple lifestyle. Parents should spend a lot of time with their children, even if it means taking time off from work. To really love a child doesn't mean that you take him or her to amusement parks; it means that you take the time to teach the child true, noble values. Only if such values are deeply ingrained in our children will they have the strength to stand firm, never weakening in adverse circumstances.

Children need to enjoy their mother's love and affection, at least until the age of five. From then till the age of fifteen, children need both love and discipline. Peace and harmony can be maintained in society only through the efforts of all parents to nurture truly good values in their children.

The integrity of each individual forms the foundation of a noble culture for the entire nation. Today's child should develop into tomorrow's mature personality. We harvest tomorrow what we sow today.

Question – Can parents send their children to *gurukulas* to be educated now, as in the past?

Mother – Materialism has replaced the spiritual culture of old. The pleasure-seeking consumer culture of today has become so firmly rooted that it is no longer possible to turn back—it is twice as strong as our traditional culture. It has gone so far that it would be meaningless to think we can uproot materialism and bring back the old way of life. Such attempts would only lead to disappointment. In today's world we need to focus on how to move forward while preventing the total decay of our values.

Living expenses have increased tremendously and it is difficult to support a family without both husband and wife working. What troubles parents the most is the education of their children. Getting a good education may be impossible without relying on private schools. But admissions and other expenses cost a great deal. To maintain their reputation, private schools teach children systematically. The sole criterion for the student's success lies in the grades secured in examinations, and has little to do with any real knowledge, wisdom, or purity of conduct.

Today's educational system places children under tremendous pressure. A new car shouldn't be driven too fast; the brand-new engine should gradually be eased into its full capacity. Otherwise, it could be damaged. Similarly, subjecting young minds to a lot of tension will damage their health and stunt their development.

Today, in the name of education, we place a heavier burden on our children than they should bear at such a tender age. At a time when children should laugh and play with their friends, we force them into the confines of classrooms, just like birds in a cage. If the child fails to get top grades in class from kindergarten onwards, the parents fret and complain. But it is the child who has to go through all that misery, not the parents. If you ask children why they are studying, most of them will reply, "To become an engineer or a doctor." Their parents prod them toward that goal from the first grade onwards. Parents seldom encourage their children to learn the true goal of life and to live accordingly.

Consider the goal of education. It is true that with a modern education you can get a degree, secure a good job and earn money—but can you attain peace of mind through that alone? These days, education is only for the purpose of attaining money and power. But, my children, do not forget that purifying the mind is the very foundation of peace and happiness in life. Only through an understanding of spirituality can we achieve that refinement to the highest degree. If we don't help our children to cultivate mental refinement and noble values, along with a modern education, we will be raising Ravanas (demons) instead of Ramas (gods).

If you walk ten times through a grass-covered area, a

clear path will form. But regardless of how many times you walk over a rock, no path will be created. Similarly, when you impart noble values to a young mind, those values will quickly make a deep impression. When the child grows up, those values will guide him or her.

Clay can be molded into any desired shape before it is placed in a kiln. But once it is fired, the shape cannot be changed. Thus we should teach our children noble values before their minds are firmly set by their exposure to the heat of worldliness. Unfortunately, the circumstances that allow us to form our children's characters are becoming increasingly limited. That is why Mother is stressing this point.

Question – Why are family relationships weakening today?

Mother – Greed and the desire for sense pleasures are growing stronger because of the influence of our materialistic culture. The moral influence women once had on men is lost. Over time, people became selfish in their craving for worldly gains. Wives began to feel forced into submission by their husbands. Mutual anger and conflicts arose. Parents who should have helped their children to develop good character sowed the poisonous seeds of selfishness and competition instead. Today we see those negative qualities in their fiercest forms. They have sprouted, grown, and spread their branches far and wide. To free ourselves from those negative qualities, what we need more than so-called equality between men and women is an understanding between men and women of each other's roles within the family. Money alone cannot give us peace. No one has ever been able to develop a pure character or inner strength with money. How can parents, who themselves do not know contentment, inculcate and nurture values such as mutual understanding and forgiveness in their children? Because of the parents' inability to properly mold their children, the power of destructive forces in society grows stronger with each generation. If we wish to change this, parents have to nurture spiritual principles in their own lives.

A child may get love from society in a variety of ways. There may be many people who are affectionate toward the child. But none of that can equal the love of a mother. A car can run on petrol, but it needs a battery to get started. For the child, the love of his or her parents is like a battery. The parental love received in childhood gives us the strength to face all circumstances in life with mental control.

There is selfishness behind the love we receive from the world. The cow is loved for the milk she provides, not out of any true love. Regardless of how much milk she has given us, once her milk dries up she is destined for the slaughterhouse. If a husband or wife doesn't yield to the other's wishes, divorce quickly follows. But a mother's love for her baby isn't rooted in any selfishness.

Apart from receiving an education and finding a job, we should also acquire an understanding of the spiritual principles. As we enter family life, our knowledge of those principles will help us take each step along the right path. My children, this is the only way to find peace. Even after eating a full meal, we still need peace of mind to sleep well.

If we build a house in a muddy area without first lay-ing a firm foundation, even a gentle wind could cause the house to collapse. Similarly, if we base our family life only on materialism, the relationships within the family could crumble when the family is faced with even small problems. But if we build our family life on the solid foundation of spirituality, we can weather any storm. This is the benefit of leading a family life based on an understanding of the true principles. There should be no lapse on the part of parents in explaining spiritual principles to their children and acting as role models.

Despite the amount of wealth that exists in developed countries, mental disease is on the rise. Only through understanding what is everlasting and what is transitory can we progress in life without ever losing our mental balance or peace of mind. Otherwise, the encroachment of materialism that we are experiencing today will cause an increase of mental illnesses in India as well. Mother will give an example. There was a family of three—father, mother, and son. The father was a high official and the mother a social worker. The son, a college student, was crazy about cricket. The family owned just one car. One evening, the father had to go to a meeting. As he started the car, his wife came out. She had been invited to a wedding and wanted to use the car. An argument erupted. At that point, the son came to the car, saying that there was a cricket match that evening, and that he needed the car to get there. All three started arguing and were soon shouting at each other. In the end, it was too late for any of them to go anywhere. All they had done was fight with each other. If, instead, the three had tried to accommodate one another, there would have been no need for an argument.

They could have shared the car and gone together. The husband could have driven his wife to the wedding, dropped off his son at the cricket field, and then gone on to his meeting. But because of their egos, all three missed their events. Instead of harmony, only anger and resentment existed among them.

Now, let us look at our own lives, my children. Are we not wasting much of our time in this way, arguing about trivial matters?

We need to grasp this point. Cultivating a spirit of humility and forgiveness and adjusting to one another's needs will strengthen our family relations day by day. In a true family, there is a sense of mutual acceptance between the husband and wife. This expands the world they share with each other, and that world grows larger still as they have children. But its boundary shouldn't stop there. It should expand even further until it embraces all sentient and insentient beings. This is the ultimate aim of family life. This is how men and women can discover their own perfection. A world of such all-encompassing love is a world of permanent happiness. It is a life without arguments or battles about yesterday, a life without meaningless worries about tomorrow. Each person lives, not with the thought "for me," but with the attitude "for you!" God appears of His own accord to grace the shrine of the family where the light of love shines brightly.

The Immortal Discourse

In March 1995, Mother and the ashram residents were on their way back to Amritapuri after the installation ceremony at the Brahmasthanam Temple[9] in Delhi. The journey took a week. Even while traveling, Mother made sure that the daily routine of Her children's spiritual practice wasn't broken. After traveling all day, the party would stop at a river or lake as dusk approached. After bathing, everyone would gather around Mother to meditate and sing bhajans.

On the evening of the third day of travel, they searched but couldn't find a river or pond on either side of the road. Noticing that everyone was getting anxious that they might not get a chance to swim that day, Mother said, "We won't miss our swim, children! That won't happen. There will be water somewhere." She stopped the bus at a certain place. When asked, the local people said, "There is no river or lake here. Water is scarce in this area." Hearing this, Mother consoled everyone, saying, "No, no—Mother's mind says there is water close by. You go and ask them again!" The brahmacharis went and asked again. Then some of the local residents remembered, "Oh, yes! There's a quarry nearby. Where the stones were cut and removed, it has become filled with water, like a small lake."

9 Brahmasthanam Temples are unique temples that Mother has established throughout India and abroad.

Mother and the group followed their directions and walked a short distance, coming upon two lakes filled with clear water. They all swam with Mother to their hearts' content. Afterwards, the group gathered around Mother to meditate, and then they joined Her in singing bhajans. At this point Mother went into a state of rapture. She raised Her arms to the sky and cried out loud, "Come quickly, children! Come running!" For a while everyone sat in silence, immersed in bliss. Then, breaking the deep silence, a Frenchman named Daniel said to Mother, "Mother, we feel great joy when swimming with you. It feels as if we have gone to the Himalayas and bathed in the Ganges. When Mother's program in Rishikesh was cancelled, we felt so disappointed at the thought of losing our chance to bathe in the Ganges. Now, that feeling is gone."

Mother – My children, temples and holy waters help bring ordinary people to spirituality, but only until they find a satguru (realized master). One who has surrendered to a satguru need not go in search of any holy river. A perfect mahatma is the confluence of all holy rivers. To fully surrender to a master is equal to bathing in all of the holy rivers.

There is a saying, that the guru's abode is Benares and the water used for washing the guru's feet is the Ganges. Indeed, the water that touches the feet of a mahatma is "Ganges water." The *pada puja* water[10] is filled with the mahatma's energy. If one drinks the pada puja water, it is not necessary to go to Benares or anywhere else. There is nothing more purifying than pada puja water—it is the real Ganges.

10 The water in which the guru's feet have been ceremonially washed.

Question – Mother, how did the waters of the sacred rivers acquire such holiness and purity?

Mother – All rivers begin from the mountains. There is no difference between the waters flowing in those rivers. What, then, is the difference between the Ganges and other rivers? Why don't you catch any diseases from bathing in the Ganges?[11]

Many mahatmas bathe in rivers like the Ganges and the Narmada, and many ascetics meditate on their banks. This creates the sacredness of these holy rivers. A river becomes holy when mahatmas bathe in it. Their pure vibrations merge with the water. Bathing in the company of a mahatma is like tasting a little of the bliss of Brahman (the Absolute Reality, Supreme Being). Bathing anywhere in the presence of a mahatma is like bathing in the Ganges.

However, faith is the foundation of everything. With love and faith, any water can become holy. Do you know the story of Pakkanar? A Brahmin was about to visit Benares. He invited Pakkanar to go with him to bathe in the Ganges and to have darshan of Lord Vishwanath of Benares. But Pakkanar couldn't go. He said, "As you are going anyway, I'd be greatly obliged if you could immerse my walking stick in the holy Ganges and bring it back to me." The Brahmin agreed and took the stick with him to Benares. In Benares, while he was bathing in the Ganges, the stick was swept away by the current. When the Brahmin returned, he explained to Pakkanar how he lost the stick. Pakkanar said to him, "Don't worry! I will get the stick back." He then took a dip in a pond near his home and

11 Here Mother is referring to all the sewage and pollution that is poured into the Ganges nowadays, the millions of people who bathe in her, and the many corpses that are placed in the water.

emerged from the water with the same stick! He said to the Brahmin, "If you have enough faith, any water can become the holy Ganges; and without faith, the Ganges and Yamuna are nothing but ordinary water."

Question – So, when Mother is with us, all the holy waters are right here. Yet, some people went to Rishikesh and Haridwar.[12]

Mother – Their surrender is limited. Once you know a mahatma, you should have the innocent faith and surrender of a child. If someone goes in search of holy waters and sacred places even after coming to a spiritual master, it means that the person's faith is not yet firm. You can get everything you need from a *satguru*; there is no need to go anywhere in search of anything.

Have you heard Ganesha's story? Ganesha and Muruga saw their mother Devi Parvati (the Divine Mother) holding a beautiful fruit in Her hand. They both asked Her for it. The Divine Mother promised the fruit to the one who first managed to complete a trip around the world. Muruga mounted his peacock and set off immediately. But Ganesha, knowing that the entire universe existed within His divine parents, did not go anywhere. He circumambulated His parents and asked His mother for the fruit. The Goddess gladly gave it to Him. The one who knew that the whole of creation existed in Shiva and Parvati, the Father and Mother of the universe, received the fruit of immortality. In the same way, if you take refuge in a satguru, everything will be given to you. All the deities and all the

12 When Mother cancelled Her trip to the Himalayas, a few disappointed western devotees went to Rishikesh and Haridwar (two holy places in the Himalayan foothills) on their own.

worlds are contained in the holy feet of the satguru. Once you have developed faith in the spiritual master, do not allow your faith to be shaken. Your faith should be immovable and ceaseless.

Moving closely with Mother is not always easy. You may experience some pain and hardships. As soon as you have to face a few minor difficulties, you may want to leave; one of you may want to go to Benares, another to Haridwar or the Himalayas to do spiritual practice. But, my children, you are unaware of the way a mahatma works on you. You do not understand and thus are thrown by this. Mother operates from the inside, very deeply, without making any external incisions. Mother operates and makes deep transformations. She removes your *vasanas* (innate tendencies) in subtle ways. You don't see this. It may be necessary to remove many things. Mother is removing the pus from the wounds within you, and this will occasionally be painful.

Mother has to extract many things. It is similar to a magnet moving beneath a tabletop. Some iron particles are lying on top of the table and it is only these you see—you cannot see the magnet. When the magnet moves, the particles on the table move and rearrange themselves, without your being able to understand how or why. You don't understand and because the process is painful you may want to run away.

Your vasanas die rapidly in the presence of a satguru. When all the vasanas die, realization happens.

My children, if you do spiritual practice by yourself, you won't necessarily be able to take away the *prarabdha*[13]

13 The fruit of past actions from this and past lives, which will manifest in this life.

of a hundred lives, but if you stay in the presence of a satguru and do spiritual practice, the prarabdha of a thousand lives can be removed.

Doing spiritual practice in the presence of a satguru is like digging a small hole near a river—you will definitely find water. Doing spiritual practice by yourself, without a master to guide you, is like digging for water in a rock.

A disciple who has totally surrendered to a spiritual master won't leave the master. The thought to leave won't even arise. Even if God comes, the disciple will stay with the master rather than go with God; the disciple will choose the master over God.

Once, there was a great sage who had many disciples. One day he summoned them all and announced: "Due to the fruits of my past actions, this body will soon become afflicted with leprosy and blindness. I will go to Benares to stay there. Is there one among you who is willing to come with me and serve me during the days of suffering that lie ahead?"

The disciples looked at each other with expressions of shock and alarm, but no one said anything. Then, the youngest disciple stood up and said, "Respected Master, I will come with you."

But the master replied, "Son, you are too young and don't yet know what it means to serve."

The youth said, "Revered Master, I am ready and will definitely come with you!"

The master tried to dissuade him, but the disciple would not give in—so intense was his desire to serve his master. And so the master and his young disciple traveled to Benares.

Soon after they arrived, the master contracted the terrible

disease and lost his eyesight. Day in and day out the disciple devotedly served his master. He never left the master alone except when he went begging for their food or washed his master's clothes. He was constantly engaged in looking after his master and made every effort to meet even his smallest needs.

In spite of the youth's unshakable devotion and utter dedication, the master often scolded him severely and accused him of making mistakes he hadn't committed. He would scold him, telling him that the clothes were not properly washed or that the food was rotten. At other times, however, the master was very loving and tender, saying that he was putting him through so much trouble.

One day Lord Shiva appeared to the disciple and said, "I am very pleased with your devotion and dedication to your master. You may ask for a boon." But the disciple didn't want to ask for anything without first receiving his master's permission. So, he ran back to his master, prostrated to him, and said, "My revered Guru, may I ask Lord Shiva for the boon to remove your disease?"

The master angrily replied, "You are not my disciple but my enemy! Is it your wish to make me suffer more by having to be born again? Don't you want me to exhaust my prarabdha now and become liberated in this lifetime?"

The disciple sadly returned to Lord Shiva and said, "O Lord, forgive me but my master won't permit me to ask for the one thing I wish. And as for me, there is nothing that I want for myself."

The years went by and the disciple, who was the embodiment of devotion, continued to serve his master with the same amount of love and unwavering surrender. One day, while the disciple was on his way to town to beg for food, Lord Vishnu appeared to him and said, "My child, I am very pleased with your devotion and dedication to your master. I am ready to give you whatever boon you ask for. You did not ask Lord Shiva for anything. Do not disappoint Me as well."

The disciple asked the Lord, "Even though I haven't served You, and I haven't even remembered You each day, how is it that You are pleased with my service?"

Lord Vishnu smiled at him and said, "There is no difference between God and the guru—God and the guru are one. It is your service to your master that pleases me."

Again the disciple sought his master's permission to ask for a boon. The master told him, "If you want a boon for yourself, go ahead and ask. But don't ask for anything on my account."

The disciple returned to Lord Vishnu and said, "O Lord, give me more knowledge and wisdom, so that I can better understand how to serve my master according to his wishes. Most of the time, due to my ignorance, I fail to understand what he likes. O Lord, grant me the knowledge to serve my master properly." Lord Vishnu was pleased and said, "So be it."

When the disciple returned to the master, the master asked him what boon he had sought from the Lord. The disciple described everything that had happened.

Suddenly, all the symptoms of leprosy vanished from the master's body and his eyesight was instantly restored. He smiled at his astounded disciple and embraced him.

The leprosy and blindness were self-imposed by that mahatma in order to test the devotion and dedication of his youngest disciple. Being ever established in the Supreme Truth, the master never had any prarabdha to work out. He blessed his disciple with supreme knowledge and said, "I am very pleased with your devotion. No harm or danger will come to those disciples who serve their master with as much devotion and dedication as you have shown me. May all disciples and their disciples in the ages to come be blessed because of you."

Children, now you are like little babies. You play and laugh with Mother, enjoying Her company. But you do not understand what Mother is doing or who Mother really is. You look only at the external Mother; hardly anyone is interested in the Supreme Consciousness that lies behind—there is no urgency to know the Self within. You don't really want the real Mother.

When a baby cries, the mother puts a pacifier in the baby's mouth, and the baby sucks on it. What a hungry baby really needs is milk. But here, babies feel content with sucking milkless pacifiers. The external world is like a pacifier. You children feel satisfied with the laughter and the play. You amuse yourselves with the objects of the senses. Mother comes to where you children are playing and puts food in your mouths. Because you are so engrossed in your play, you don't appreciate the value of the food that Mother gives you. You won't advance if you just keep wandering around visiting temples and holy places.

My children, you should cultivate the spirit of innocence. Your innocence and purity of heart will save you. Anything is possible with the faith and trust of a child.

Question – But we don't have that innocence, do we,

Mother? Haven't we lost that childlike heart?

Mother – No, you haven't lost that innocence. It is still there within you. Don't you spontaneously become childlike when you play with a little child? You go to that level. When you put food in a child's mouth, don't you also open your mouth to be fed, like a child? When we play with children, we forget everything and become like them. We rejoice with children. We forget our selfishness because we become one with the innocent hearts of the children.

But the head so often stands in the way of the heart. We must relinquish the rational mind and dive deeply into the heart. Embrace the heart, my children. If a mixture of sugar and sand is left lying around, ants will come and nibble only on the sugar. They will enjoy the sweetness. But a human being, who functions from the intellect, is not able to do that. He or she just scratches at everything with the intellect. To savor the sweetness, we need to open up our hearts.

Question – Mother, without being aware of it, we go where the mind tells us to go. What can we do about this?

Mother – My children, until now you have placed your faith in the mind. But the mind is like a monkey that jumps from branch to branch, from one thought to another, and will continue to do this until its last moment. The mind will remain present until the very end. Making the mind your companion is like befriending a fool—it will always create some trouble; you will never find any peace. If we keep the company of fools, we will also become fools. It is foolish to put your trust in the mind and to follow the mind. Don't get trapped by the mind. We should always remember the goal—Self-realization. We shouldn't allow ourselves to be led astray by any distractions along the way.

You carry all your samskaras with you, so you have to proceed little by little, step by step. It is a slow process which needs faith and confidence. It is important to be detached from your thoughts and to refuse to get carried away by the mind.

Question – Amma, bad thoughts keep arising in the mind however hard I try not to think them.

Mother – Don't be afraid! Don't give any importance to such thoughts when they arise. Suppose we travel on a pilgrimage by bus. We watch the scenery through the window—some of it is beautiful, some not. But regardless of how intriguing the sights before us are, we forget them as soon as the bus has passed them by. We don't stop the bus every time we spot something beautiful. We appreciate the beauty, but we continue forward without stopping, keeping our minds on the goal. Otherwise, we will never arrive. We need to focus on our destination. Let the thoughts and vasanas that arise in your mind pass by like the scenery through the bus window. Don't allow yourself to be captured by them. Then, they won't affect you that much.

There are two sides to the mind. One side looks intently toward the goal and yearns for realization. The other side looks only at the outer world. There is a battle raging between the two. As long as you don't identify with or give any importance to the thoughts that arise in the mind, there is no problem.

At present your mind resembles a mirror on the roadside, reflecting whatever passes by along the road. In the same way, the mind goes out toward whatever we see or hear.

Yet, we lack one quality that the mirror has: even though the mirror reflects everything clearly, nothing affects it; everything vanishes as soon as it passes out of view. The mirror is not attached to anything. This is what our minds should be like. We should let go of whatever we see, hear, or think about, then and there—like a passing sight along the road. We shouldn't be attached to anything. We should know that the thoughts that rise and fall belong to the mind but do not affect the Self. Live as a mere witness.

If you wish to enjoy the beauty of a swiftly flowing river—not only the water, but also the fish and other creatures and things that dwell in the water, everything comprising the nature of a river—it is best to sit beside the river and observe it. If you jump into the water, you may get carried away by the current and even drown, and you won't be able to experience the beauty of the river. Similarly, live like a witness, without getting caught in the flow of the mind. Learn to detach from it.

We should control the mind and have the power to stop it—like the brakes of a new car, which control the speed and stop the vehicle whenever necessary.

People have faith in their minds but not in the spiritual master. But to trust the mind is like placing yourself at the mercy of a fool. The mind is foolish. It enjoys reflecting only the surface of everything it sees, without comprehending the deeper truth.

Satsang—being in the presence of a great soul, reading spiritual books, and listening to spiritual discourses—is very important. These activities will help develop your power of discrimination and bring you peace. Personal effort is also necessary.

The path we must tread is full of hurdles. We need to always be vigilant, as if crossing a bridge unused for a long time and covered with slippery mud. We risk falling at any moment, and thus must be very attentive at each step. Should we happen to fall, we have to pick ourselves up. The fall actually occurs so that we can train ourselves to pick ourselves up. Victory and defeat are the very nature of life. From now on, take every step with greater caution. It is no good being in a difficult or negative situation without doing anything about it. Know that the risk of falling will remain until the last moment, right up till the eve of liberation.

We must use our discrimination when desires, anger, and jealousy arise in the mind. Be vigilant as you go forward, my children, because you could fall at any moment.

Question – In case we should fall, will Mother help us to get up again?

Mother – Know that Mother is always with you. Have faith. My children, there is no need to be afraid. But effort and perseverance are necessary on your part. If you call Mother with innocence and faith, She is always ready to help you. If you fall, rise up again. Turn the fall into an ascent.

Question – Do Self-realized mahatmas have any likes or dislikes?

Mother – No, in that state everything is the same; there are no preferences. There is only the observing witness. A mahatma is the master of his or her mind and can always say no. If the mahatma wants to play the game, he or she uses the mind to do so—but can control it, break if off, at any moment. The mind of a mahatma resembles the brakes of an expensive car: when you apply the brakes, even at great speed, the car stops immediately and doesn't skid.

Ordinary people are controlled by their minds; they move only as their minds direct them. But a mahatma holds a firm grip on his or her mind; the mind has no power over the mahatma. The mahatma simply witnesses everything. Mother is talking here about real mahatmas—not about those who go around claiming that they are free of all bonds, while still harboring desires and anger within.

Interviews with the Divine Mother

(*An interview given by Mother for an English language magazine*)

Question – What is the message of Mother's life?

Mother – Mother's life is Her message—and that is love.

Question – Those who have met you never tire of praising your love. Why is this so?

Mother – Mother doesn't deliberately show any special love toward anyone. Love just happens, naturally and spontaneously. Mother cannot dislike anyone. She knows only one language, and that is the language of love. It is the one language everyone understands. The greatest poverty experienced in the world today is the lack of selfless love.

All people speak about love and say that they love each other. But that cannot be called real love. What people today think of as love is tainted with selfishness, like a cheap ornament plated with gold. It may be nice to wear but it is of poor quality and won't last long.

There is a story about a little girl who got sick and was admitted to the hospital. When it was time for her to go home, she said to her father, "Dad, the people here are so good to me! Do you love me as much as they do? The doctor and nurses have been looking after me—they all love me so much! They ask me how I'm feeling. They take care of all my needs; they make my bed, they feed me on time, and they never scold me. You and Mom are always scolding me!" Just then, the receptionist handed a piece of paper to the father. The girl asked what it was. The father said, "Weren't you just telling me how much these people love you? Well, this is the bill for that love!"

My children, this shows the nature of the love we find in today's world. Some form of selfishness hides behind all the love that we see. The trading mentality of the marketplace has crept into individual relationships. The first thought that arises in people's minds when they meet someone is what they can gain from that person. If there is nothing to be gained, they don't bother to build a relationship. And when in a relationship, as soon as the gains decrease, the relationship wanes as well. This is how much selfishness there is in people's minds. Humanity is suffering now as a consequence.

These days, if there are three members in a family, it is as if they live on three separate islands. The world has degenerated to such an extent that people no longer know what real peace and harmony are. This has to change. Selflessness has to flourish instead of selfishness. People should stop bargaining with one another in the name of relationships. Love shouldn't be a chain of bondage; it should be the very breath of life. This is Mother's wish.

Once we develop the attitude that "I am love, the embodiment of love," then we need not wander in search of peace; for peace will come in search of us. In that expansive state of mind, all conflicts dissolve, just as the mist fades when the sun rises.

Question – Someone has said, "If you want to know what love would look like if it were to take on a human form, you need only look at Mother!" Could Mother say something about this?

Mother – (Laughs) If you give someone ten rupees out of the hundred you have, only ninety rupees will remain. But love is different. No matter how much love you give, it can never be exhausted. The more you give, the more you will have, like an endless spring that flows into the well as you draw water. Mother knows only this much: that Her life should be a message of love. This is Mother's only concern. People are born to be loved. They live for love. Yet, it is the one thing not available today. A famine of love plagues the world.

Question – Mother gives solace to all people who come to Her by holding each one of them in Her arms. Isn't this unconventional in India?

Mother – Don't mothers lift their babies up and hug them? Our country has always glorified the mother-child relationship. Mother doesn't see those who come to Her as different or separate from Herself. If there is pain in any part of your body, your hand will instinctively move there to give comfort. To Mother, the sorrows and sufferings of others are Her own. Can a mother who sees her child crying in pain just stand by and watch?

Question – Mother, do you love the poor and forsaken more than you love others?

Mother – Mother doesn't know how to be partial in Her love. If a lamp is lit in front of a house, everyone who comes there will receive an equal amount of light, neither more nor less than anyone else. But if you keep the doors closed and stay inside, you will continue to be in the dark. To remain in the dark and then to blame the light is of no use. If you want the light, you have to open the doors of the heart and come out.

The sun doesn't need a candle to light its way. Some people believe that God is someone sitting somewhere up in the sky. They spend money lavishly to please God. But God's grace cannot be obtained just by spending money. Serving the poor is dearer to God than anything. God is far more pleased when He sees a poor person being helped and comforted, than when millions are spent on an ostentatious religious festival. God's grace pours forth when He sees you wiping the tears of a suffering soul. Wherever God beholds such a pure mind, there He hastens to dwell. A compassionate heart is a far more precious dwelling place to God than any silken couch or golden throne.

Mother looks only at Her children's hearts. She doesn't judge them by their material circumstances or status in the world. No real mother would think about such things. But when a sorrowful person comes to Mother, She is filled with compassion at the sight of that grief. Mother will feel that person's sorrow as Her own and will do whatever She can to comfort him or her.

Question – Doesn't Mother get tired, spending so much time with Her devotees?

Mother – Where there is love, there is no tiredness. A mother carries her child for hours on end. Does she think of her child as a burden?

Question – In the early days Mother had to face a lot of opposition. Could Mother say something about that?

Mother – It didn't seem that important to Mother. Mother knew the nature of the world. Say that you are watching a fireworks display. If you know that a very loud firecracker is about to go off, you won't get startled when it explodes. Those who know how to swim in the sea will enjoy playing amidst the waves and won't let fear weaken them. Since Mother already knew the nature of the world, the obstacles in Her life didn't mar Her inner joy. She felt that those who opposed Her were like mirrors. They prompted Her to look inward. That was Mother's attitude toward them.

Complaints and sorrows arise only when you think you are the body. In the realm of the Self there is no place for sorrow. When Mother contemplated the nature of the Self, it became clear to Her that She was not a stagnant pond, but a free-flowing river.

Many people come to the river—the sick as well as the healthy. Some drink from the water; others bathe in it, wash their clothes in it, or even spit in it. It makes no difference to the river how people treat it—it keeps flowing. Whether the water is used for worship or for bathing, it never complains. It flows along, caressing and purifying those who enter it. But the water of a pond is stagnant and unclean, and will inevitably have a foul smell.

Once Mother recognized this, neither the opposition She faced, nor the love She received could affect Her in the least. None of it seemed important. Sorrow arises when you think, "I am the body." There is no room for sorrow on the plane of the Self. No one was separate from Mother. To Mother, the shortcomings of others were Her own. So, those hardships didn't seem like hardships to Mother. They threw dirt at this tree, but for Mother it turned into fertilizer. Everything was for the ultimate good.

Question – Mother, are you not experiencing the Self? Why, then, do you pray? What is the need for spiritual practice in Mother's case?

Mother – Mother has taken this body for the sake of the world, not for Herself. Mother has not come to this world just to sit, declaring, "I am a divine incarnation." What is the use being born if you sit idle? Mother's aim is to guide people and thereby to uplift the world. Mother has come with the aim of showing people the right path.

With people who are deaf we use sign language to communicate, don't we? If we think, "I am not deaf, so why should I make those signs with my hands?" then the deaf won't be able to understand anything we say. For them, such gestures are necessary. Similarly, to uplift those who are ignorant of their true nature, one has to come down to their level. One shows them, by living among them and by setting an example with one's own life, that they need to sing devotional songs, meditate, and do selfless service—everything. For the sake of uplifting people, Mother assumes many roles. All these roles are played for the sake of the world.

People come to the ashram by car, bus, plane, or boat. Mother doesn't ask, "What type of vehicle did you use to get here?" She doesn't say, "You should come only by plane!" Each person uses the means most suitable for him or her. Likewise, many paths lead to Self-realization. Mother prescribes for each person the path suitable for his or her mental disposition. Those who have an aptitude for mathematics should choose one of the sciences at college. They will be able to learn those subjects more easily than others and will quickly advance in their studies. Those with the intellectual ability to grasp the meaning of scriptural texts may be able to meditate on "Not this, not this" (*neti, neti*) on the intellectual level and make progress. However, it requires a subtle intellect and considerable knowledge of the scriptures to achieve this. An ordinary person won't succeed.

Many people who visit the ashram for the first time are not even familiar with the word, "spirituality." What will such children do? You need a certain level of education or contact with a spiritual master to really understand books like the Bhagavad Gita. Those who don't have any of this also need to make progress, don't they? Only those who really have the power of discrimination can take the path of "neti, neti." And only those who have studied the scriptures will be able to find the scriptural words to suit every situation and contemplate them deeply. Very few can do this. How can Mother reject those who can't? Shouldn't they be uplifted as well? So, to uplift them, it is necessary to know the level of each person, and then to descend to that level.

Many people who come here are illiterate. There are also people who are too poor to buy books, even though they know how to read. Some who come here have acquired a little knowledge from reading. Others have read a lot, but are unable to put what they have learned into practice in their lives. Each person also needs to be guided according to the culture in which he or she grew up. Brahman is not something conveyed in words. It is pure experience—it is life. It is a state in which you see everyone as your own Self. That state should become our very nature. We become the flower, rather than contemplate the flower. We should all try to blossom. This is what we should make of our lives, and what our studies should be directed toward. Memorizing something is not that difficult; putting what you have learned into practice is difficult. The rishis (sages) of long ago demonstrated great spiritual truths through the examples of their lives. These days, people engage in verbal disputes after having read and memorized the words of the sages.

Pujas (sacred rituals) and prayer are all different facets of Brahman.

Question – Mother, in your ashram much importance is given to service. Isn't action an impediment to true contemplation of the Self?

Mother – The stairs leading up are built of bricks and cement. The top floor is also made of bricks and cement. Only when you reach the top will you know that there is no difference between the stairs and the top floor. Still, the steps are necessary to reach the top. Likewise, to attain Self-realization, certain means are necessary.

Once, a man rented a palatial building and lived there as if he were the king of the area. One day when a holy man came to see him, he behaved very arrogantly, putting on royal airs. The holy man said to him, "You say that this palace belongs to you. I suggest you ask your conscience the truth. You yourself know that this is only a rented building. There is nothing here that you can call your own; you don't own a single item in this house. Yet you imagine everything is yours and that you are a king!" This is what most people are like today. They read numerous books and blabber about what they have read, like crows cawing on the beach.[14] What they speak of has no resemblance whatsoever to the lives they lead. Those who have understood the scriptures even a little don't waste their time arguing. They will only advise those who approach them, and will try to help them advance.

Each person needs a path best suited to his or her mental disposition. This is why there are so many paths in Sanatana Dharma, the Eternal Religion. The paths begin at the level of each person and are designed to take each individual upwards. *Advaita* (non-duality) is not to be crammed into the brain—it is to be lived. Only then can it be experienced.

Some people come here claiming to be experts in Vedanta. They claim to be Pure Consciousness. They ask, "Where is there another Self for the Self to serve? What is the need for service in an ashram where aspirants strive for Self-realization? Surely, studying and contemplation are enough!" In the olden days, even the great souls embraced vanaprastha[15] and *sannyasa* only after they had gone through grihasthashrama (a spiritually oriented family life). Most

---

14 In many parts of Kerala the beaches are populated with crows.

15 Vanaprastha is traditionally the third stage of life, when the husband and wife retire to the forest for spiritual practice, leaving behind all worldly responsibilities.

of their karmic prarabdha (the work one must do to exhaust one's karmic debts) was exhausted by then, and they had only a limited number of days left to live. In the ashrams they visited there was plenty of selfless service. There, the disciples, who were students of *Vedanta*, would serve Vedantic masters with complete surrender. The disciples would go out to collect firewood and tend the cows. Haven't you heard the story of Aruni, who protected the fields? To prevent water from flooding into the field through a break in a levee and destroying the crops, he laid himself down against the levee and stopped the flow. For those disciples, nothing was separate from Vedanta. Aruni didn't think, "This is just a field, all mud and dirt. I, on the other hand, am the Self." For him everything was the Self.

That is what the disciples were like in those days. There was karma yoga (selfless service) even then. Only three or four disciples lived with a spiritual master in those days.

This ashram has nearly a thousand residents. Are they able to meditate all the time? No. Thoughts will creep into their minds even then. Whether they work or not, a lot of thoughts arise in their minds. So, why not channel those thoughts in the right direction, using our arms and legs to do some selfless service for the benefit of others?

Lord Krishna said to Arjuna, "O Arjuna, in all the three worlds, there is nothing I need to do, nothing for me to attain, and yet I am ever engaged in action." Children, your minds are stuck at the level of body-consciousness. Your minds need to be lifted above that. Let your minds expand and become the universal Mind. Compassion toward the world will produce the first shoots of that growth.

Those who proudly claim to be Vedantins believe that

they alone are Brahman, and that everything else is maya, illusion. But are they able to maintain that attitude? Never! They expect lunch to be ready at exactly twelve or one o'clock. They don't think of food as maya when they are hungry! And when they get sick they want to be taken to the hospital. At that time the hospital isn't maya; it is a necessity and they need the service rendered by others.

Those who talk about maya and pure consciousness should understand that, just as they themselves need certain things, those same things are also essential for others. Those so-called Vedantins need the service of others. To expect others to serve you, and then to start contemplating Brahman when it is time to serve others is just a sign of laziness.

In this ashram, there are doctors and engineers and people of many other professions. Everyone works according to his or her capacity. But the residents here also meditate and study the scriptures. They train themselves to perform actions without any attachment. Working without attachment helps us to get rid of selfishness and body-consciousness. When an action is done without attachment, it doesn't cause any bondage. That is the path to liberation.

None of the residents here at the ashram have any desire for heaven. Ninety percent of them want to serve the world. Even if offered heaven, they will just wave it goodbye, because they already experience heaven in their hearts. They have no need for any other heaven. Their heaven is their own compassionate hearts. This is the attitude of most of Mother's children here.

Many people have withdrawn from society in the past,

claiming to be Pure Consciousness. They were not prepared to go out among people and serve them. This explains why our civilization has degenerated to such a degree. What we suffer today is the misery caused by all that indifference. With your question, do you mean to say that we should allow our culture to be impoverished even further?

It should be understood that advaita is something to be lived. It is a state in which we look upon all others as our own Self.

What is the meaning of the Kurukshetra War? When rough stones are put into a rotating drum, the stones lose their sharp edges and become smooth. In the same way, by serving the world, the mind loses its deformity and attains the nature of the Self—the individual consciousness becomes one with the Universal Consciousness. By serving the world you battle the negativities within you, such as the ego and all your selfishness. That is the true meaning of the Mahabharata War and why the Lord asked Arjuna to fight for the sake of dharma.

If you adhere to these teachings through your actions, others will more clearly understand than if you try to explain the teachings in words. This is Mother's aim.

Question – Mother, in your ashram, do you accord the greatest importance to devotion? When I watch the prayers and devotional singing, it seems almost like a show.

Mother – Son, say you have a girlfriend. If you were talking to her, would it seem like a show to you? If there is real love, you will never think like that. To someone else, however, it may appear to be a show. The same is true here as well. To us, this could never be a show. Our prayers are expressions of our bond with God. During each moment of our prayers, we experience nothing but bliss. Whether the lover talks to his beloved, or she talks to him, it gives them joy. They won't feel any discontentment. They won't feel bored even after hours of talking to each other. We experience a similar enjoyment when we pray.

Prayer is a dialogue with the Beloved within ourselves—our true Self.

You are that Self, the atman. You are not meant to be unhappy, ever. You are not the individual soul. You are the Supreme Being. Your nature is bliss. This is the purpose of prayer. Real prayer is not just empty words.

Son, if by devotion you mean praying and singing devotional songs, you will find that in all religions. Muslims pray and prostrate toward Mecca. The Christians pray before an image of Christ, a cross, or a burning candle. Jains, Buddhists, and Hindus also pray. In all these religions, the master-disciple relationship exists as well. We see prophets and masters appearing in our midst from time to time who are greatly revered. Aren't these different expressions of devotion? Those who have learned the scriptures meditate on the principles of Vedanta, and thus move forward on the spiritual path. Isn't it because of their devotion to those principles that they are able to do this?

Son, true devotion is to see God in everyone, and to be respectful toward everyone. We should cultivate this attitude. Our minds should be uplifted so that we see the Divine in everything. Here in India we don't imagine God as residing in a heaven. God is everywhere. Nothing is more important in life than to know God. The aim of hearing scriptural truths, contemplating them, and assimilating them is to realize the nature of the supreme Being or God. Devotion is a spiritual path that leads to that same goal.

It is not easy for everyone to turn the mind inward, for the mind likes to wander in every direction. Those who have studied the scriptures may prefer the path of "neti, neti" ("not this, not this") rejecting their identification with everything except the Self. But so many people haven't studied anything. They, too, need to know the Self, don't they? For them, devotion is the most practical way.

Some people have allergic reactions to injections. They could even die if given one. When ill, they have to take oral medication instead. That alone is suitable for them. In the same way, Mother prescribes different spiritual practices for different people, depending on what suits each individual's samskara (mental disposition stemming from this life and previous lives). We can't say that this or that method is more important than others. Rather, we can say that everything here is directed toward the welfare of the people.

Because a river is filled with water, we see two riverbanks, and we talk of this side and that side. But if the river runs dry, we see that there's only a continuous stretch of sand; the two banks and the riverbed form part of the same ground. In the same way, the concept of "you" and "I" arises only because we continue to have a sense of individuality. Once the individuality disappears, everything is one and the same—whole and perfect (purnam). Through both paths, "not this, not this" and devotion, we can attain the experience of the Self.

The path of "neti, neti" can be described like this: A child is bringing medicines to his bedridden father. Just as he is about to enter the room, the power supply fails. He is suddenly in the dark and cannot see anything. He feels the wall—"that's not it." He feels the door—"not this." He feels the table—"not that." He feels the bed—"not that." Finally he touches his father. "Yes! Here he is!" In this way, by rejecting everything that is not his father, he reaches his father.

It is the same with devotion. A true devotee's attention is only on God. God is all he or she cares about. The devotee won't accept anything other than God. Only the thought of the Beloved exists.

One group of seekers says, "I am not the body, nor the mind, nor the intellect—I am the Self. The mind and body are the cause of all sorrow and happiness." Others have the attitude, "I belong to God. I need only God. God is everything." This is the only difference. We begin to see that there is nothing but God. This should be our life. We should perceive everything as God. That is real devotion. When we see only God in everything, we forget ourselves; our individuality dissolves.

Through our devotion, we are not seeking a God who sits somewhere beyond the sky; rather, we learn to see God in everything. Such a devotee doesn't need to wander about in search of God. God shines within that devotee, because he or she doesn't see anything as different from God. The purpose of prayer is to realize this state. Through our prayers we glorify Truth. The mind needs to be uplifted from the level of body, mind, and intellect to the level of the Self. Say that a hundred-watt light bulb hangs in the kitchen.

The bulb is so covered by soot that it doesn't even give the output of a ten-watt bulb. If we wipe off the soot, the bulb will once again shine with its full brilliance. Similarly, spiritual practice is the process of removing our impurities. By removing the veil that obscures our innate divinity, we will experience the infinite power within us. We will understand that we weren't born to experience sorrow, but that our true nature is bliss. However, it is not enough to simply talk about these truths. Spiritual practice is required. Everyone has the innate capacity to swim, but only if we get into the water and practice will we learn how to swim. Devotion and prayer are means by which we awaken the Divinity within us.

Question – It is said that if a spiritual aspirant touches someone, the aspirant will lose his or her spiritual power. It this true?

Mother – A small battery has only a limited amount of power and will weaken when used. But there will always be power in a wire connected to the main power supply. Similarly, you will lose your power if you believe yourself to be the limited ego, similar to a small battery. But if you are connected to God, the Source of infinite power, how can you lose any power? Only the Infinite comes out of the Infinite. Even if you light a thousand wicks from a single flame, the brightness of the original flame does not decrease at all.

It is true, however, that a spiritual aspirant can lose his or her power. You must be very alert, because you are still on the plane of body, mind, and intellect. As long as you remain on that plane, you always have to be careful.

Until the mind lies within your control, it is necessary to observe all the yamas and niyamas (do's and don'ts on the spiritual path). Afterwards, you need not worry if you happen to touch someone. Consider those you touch as God, not as people—then you won't lose strength; you will gain strength.

Question – Mother, you went through a lot of suffering in your childhood. When you see people suffer, do you remember those days?

Mother – Is there anyone who hasn't suffered in life? It is true that Mother experienced many hardships when She was young, but She didn't think of them as real hardships. Mother's mother, Damayanti, fell ill and was unable to take care of the household. Under those circumstances, Mother consoled Herself thinking that even if Her own education was interrupted, Her brothers and sisters could complete their studies. Thus She ended Her schooling and assumed complete responsibility for all household chores. She cooked for the family, prepared lunch boxes for Her brothers and sisters, washed everyone's clothes, took care of the cows, goats, ducks, chickens, and other animals, and collected grass for the cows. She also nursed Her mother Damayanti. She did one chore after another from four in the morning until midnight. Through such experiences, Mother learned firsthand, right from childhood, the meaning of hardship.

She went to at least fifty houses in the area to collect tapioca peels for the cows. One family would be eating when She arrived. In the next house, the people had nothing and would be starving. The children would be lying on the floor, weak with hunger. In one house, Mother heard the children praying for the long life of their parents, while in the neighboring house, the grandmother was totally neglected and knew nothing but despair. "Nobody looks after me," the old woman would complain. "They feed me in the same way one would feed a dog. No one helps me to wash my clothes. I only get shouted at and beaten by everyone."

This was the story of many of the elderly people. They had toiled for their children throughout their lives. They had lost their health in their struggle to provide for their children. But in their old age, as they lay there helpless, no one supported them. No one even bothered to give them a little water when they were thirsty. Seeing their suffering, Mother would bring them food from Her home.

Once they have their own families and responsibilities, the children, who once prayed for the longevity of their parents, come to think of their aged parents as a nuisance. They want to get rid of them. They love others only if they can expect to get something in return. The cow is loved for its milk. If it stops giving milk, the owner gets rid of it. Mother came to understand that there is always a selfish motive behind worldly love.

There was a pond close to our house. Mother used to bring the old women there. She would bathe them and wash their clothes. She would pick up children crying of hunger, and bring them home and feed them. Her father didn't like this. He would scold Her saying, "Why do you bring all those filthy children with runny noses here?"

By witnessing firsthand the suffering and hardships of people, Mother learned about the nature of life in the world.

When people get sick and go to the hospital, they have to wait for many hours. Finally the doctor may see them and give a prescription. But where will the money for the medicine come from? Mother has witnessed so many destitute people who don't even have the money to buy a single painkiller. The people in this area barely manage to live from day to day on their meager wages. If they miss work for just one day, the family goes hungry. If they get sick, they have no money for food or medicine. You see people writhing in pain, with no money to buy painkillers. One pill would be enough; the pain would abate in a few minutes. But there is no money even for that, and so they suffer in agony all day long.

Mother has seen many children in tears because they couldn't afford to buy paper for their examinations.[16] Some children go to school with their shirtfronts held together with thorns because they can't afford to replace the broken buttons. Thus Mother has seen, heard, and experienced the suffering and hardships that people undergo in their lives. Because of this, She understood the nature of the world. It prompted Her to look inward. Everything in the world became Her guru. Even a tiny ant was Her guru.

Because Mother shared the sorrows and the suffering of the poor while still a child, She understands people's pain and suffering without them having to explain anything. Today countless people who experience similar hardships come to see Her. If those who have the resources made up their minds, they could alleviate the suffering of these people to a great extent. Mother would like to urge

16 In some Indian schools where education is free, the students have to provide their own examination sheets. This is not the case at Mother's schools (Amrita Vidyalayams).

Her wealthy children to be compassionate and serve the poor and the suffering.

Question – How can Mother, who has never given birth, be considered a mother?

Mother – My children, the mother is a symbol of selflessness. A mother knows the heart of her child; she knows the child's feelings. She dedicates Her whole life to that child. A mother will forgive any mistakes her child makes, because she knows that he or she errs only out of ignorance. This is true motherhood. And that is what Mother's life is about. Mother sees everyone as Her own child.

Indian culture teaches children from early childhood that their mother is God, the embodiment of God. Our culture regards motherhood as the consummation of womanhood. Traditionally, every man looks upon every woman, besides his wife, as a mother. A woman also addresses all elderly women and women who deserve her respect as "mother." Such is the exalted position traditionally accorded to women in our society. Today that attitude has been lost to some extent, due to the influence of other cultures. You can see the consequence of this decline in our society.

The maternal quality is innate in every woman. This quality should be the predominant quality in all women. Just as darkness is dispelled by the rays of the sun, all undesirable tendencies disappear before the quality of motherhood. This is how pure the maternal quality is. Love, selflessness, and self-sacrifice form the hallmarks of motherhood. Only by fostering these qualities within ourselves can we keep our noble culture alive.

Mother feels that Her way is suitable for this. You ask how Mother can be a mother without ever having given birth. But doesn't the engineer who designed the engine of an airplane know more about the engine than the pilot? A woman doesn't become a mother just by giving birth; the maternal quality has to blossom within her. Similarly, a woman who has developed the mother within herself, in all its fullness, is no less a mother than a woman who has given birth to a baby. Also, do we not look upon our motherland, our mother tongue, and mother earth as mothers?

Question – Mother, are you working in society to attain a particular goal?

Mother – Mother has only one desire: that Her life should be like an incense stick. As it burns itself out, the incense stick spreads its fragrance for the benefit of others. Similarly, Mother wants to benefit the world by dedicating every moment of Her life to Her children. She does not see the goal as being different from the means. Mother's life flows according to Divine Will, that is all.

Question – It is said that a spiritual master is essential on the spiritual path. Who was Mother's guru?

Mother – Everything in this world is Mother's guru. God and the guru are within every person. But as long as the ego persists, we remain unaware of this. The ego acts like a veil and hides the inner guru. Once you discover the inner guru, you will perceive the guru in everything in the universe. As Mother found the guru within Herself, everything, including each grain of sand, became Her guru. You may wonder then if even a thorn was Mother's guru. Yes, every thorn was Her guru; for when your foot is pricked by a thorn, you pay greater attention to the path. Thus, that thorn helps you to avoid being pricked by other thorns and to avoid falling into a deep ditch.

Mother also looks upon Her body as a guru; because when we contemplate the impermanent nature of the body we come to realize that the Self is the only eternal reality. Everything around Mother led Her to goodness, and because of this, Mother feels a sense of reverence toward everything in life.

Question – Is Mother saying that we don't need a particular guru to attain Self-realization?

Mother – Mother is not saying that. A person with an inborn gift for music may be able to sing all the traditional melodic variations or ragas without any special training. But imagine if everyone else started singing ragas without any training! So, Mother doesn't say that a spiritual master isn't necessary; only that a few rare individuals gifted with an unusual degree of awareness and attentiveness have no need for an external guru.

View everything you come across with discrimination and awareness. Do not harbor any feelings of attachment or aversion toward anything. Then, everything will have something to teach you. But how many among us have that much detachment, patience, and one-pointedness? For those who haven't yet developed those qualities, it would be extremely difficult to reach the goal without taking refuge in an external guru. The real guru awakens your inner knowledge. These days people aren't able to perceive the inner guru because they are afflicted with the blindness of their ignorance. We have to transform our way of seeing in order to perceive the light of knowledge. The attitude of being a disciple, the attitude of surrender, helps you to achieve this.

We should have the attitude of a beginner. Only a beginner has the patience to really learn anything. Just because your body has grown doesn't necessarily mean that your mind has matured. If you want your mind to broaden and become as expansive as the universe, you need to have the attitude of a child; because only a child can grow and develop. But the attitude of most people has become that of the ego, of the body, mind, and intellect. Only when we discard that attitude and we assume the attitude of an innocent child, will we have the attentiveness necessary to absorb what we are taught.

No matter how much water falls on a mountaintop, the water won't stay there; it flows down naturally and fills a hole in the ground. Similarly, if we have the attitude that we are nothing, everything will come to us.

Patience, awareness, and attentiveness are the real wealth in life. A person who has gained these qualities can succeed anywhere—that is how important they are. When you develop these qualities, your internal mirror, which helps you to see the impurities within yourself and removes them, becomes clear of its own accord. You become your own mirror; you will know how to remove your impurities without needing anyone's help. You attain the ability to purify yourself. When you reach that stage, you behold the guru everywhere. You don't see anyone as inferior to yourself. You never argue unnecessarily. You don't resort to empty words. Your greatness is reflected in your actions.

Question – Does that mean that there is no need to study spiritual texts?

Mother – It is good to study Vedanta. The path to God will then quickly become clear to you. Those who study Vedanta will understand how close God is, that God is within them. But today most people limit Vedanta to mere words. We don't see any Vedanta reflected in their actions. Vedanta is not a load to be carried around; it is a principle to be brought into the heart and practiced by the mind. Many people fail to grasp this and become arrogant. As our understanding of Vedanta increases, humility develops within us naturally. Vedanta helps us to understand that we are the essence of God. However, to bring that into actual experience, we have to live by the principles of Vedanta. If you write the word "sugar" on a piece of paper and lick it, you won't experience any sweetness. To experience the sweetness, you have to taste the sugar. Mere reading or talking about Brahman won't give us the experience of Brahman. Our actions should reflect what we have read and studied. It is then that our knowledge becomes our own experience. But our efforts need some encouragement. The lives of those who have truly learned Vedanta and interiorized it inspire others to follow that same path.

Some people sit idly declaring, "I am Brahman." Why, then, did that Brahman (referring to that person) assume a body? Wasn't it enough to remain formless? Now that we have received this body, we must demonstrate that truth with our actions. Once we understand this, we will naturally be humble.

Mother is talking about Her own life. She doesn't insist that others should accept or follow it as such. You should proceed on the basis of your own experience. Know who you are! This is all Mother is saying.

(The following is an interview with Mother published in the Times of India. The interview took place during Mother's visit to New Delhi in March 1999.)

Question – Mother has founded AIMS,[17] the super-specialty hospital, and the Amrita Kuteeram free housing project, and many other service projects for the poor. What motivated Mother to start those service activities?

Mother – Mother sees many poor people every day. They tell Her about their suffering. Thus Mother has come to understand their hardships and their needs. A strong urge to alleviate their suffering is felt within. That is how each project begins. None of the projects were planned before they were started; nor had any funds been gathered. As we begin each project, God sends us everything we need.

We should understand that God is not confined to the temple or the church. God is within each one of us. Whenever we share what we have with others and help one another, we are, in fact, worshipping God.

To go to the places of worship and pray to God, and then, as we come out, to turn our face away from the starving person on the street—that is not true devotion.

17 Amrita Institute of Medical Sciences (AIMS) in Cochin, Kerala.

Question – The statements made by some philosophers regarding the individual soul and the Supreme Being have created the impression that there is no difference between God and human beings. They have also made it seem as if there is no difference between good and bad, pure and impure, or heaven and hell. Doesn't this help to blur the distinction between right and wrong?

Mother – This arises from a misunderstanding. The objective of teaching people about the principle of non-duality—the oneness of the individual soul and the Supreme Being—is to awaken the innate strength within them and lead them to the Truth. Vedanta tells us, "You are the King of kings; you are not a beggar!" This awareness about ourselves helps awaken the infinite power within us. But until we realize this oneness through direct experience, we have to discriminate between good and evil, and progress along the right path. Once you realize the ultimate Truth, the world of duality ceases to exist for you—there is only the Truth and nothing to cast aside as wrong. You see everything as a manifestation of God.

Every word and deed of such a soul benefits society. Even coming in contact with such a person's breath will help eradicate the negative tendencies within us. A person who is aware of his or her divinity will never be disturbed when confronted with the problems of the world. A real Vedantin is someone who actually lives in that state of non-duality, not someone who merely talks about it. A real Vedantin is a living example to the world.

Those who drink alcohol and do other wrong actions while quoting the scriptures, declaring that all is Brahman, cannot be considered spiritual. We should be able to recognize such hypocrites. Our inability to do so is one reason why our culture has fallen to such an extent.

Spirituality isn't something to be just talked about; it has to be lived.

Question – Can a selfish person become selfless through his or her own effort? Can we change our own nature?

Mother – Certainly. If you have a proper understanding of the spiritual principles, your selfishness will diminish. A most efficient way to decrease selfishness is to perform actions without desiring any of the fruits. We should always remember that we are just instruments in God's hands. We should know that we are not the doers, but that God is making us do everything. When we sincerely have this attitude, pride and selfishness will leave us.

A person calls from the top of the stairs, "I will be right down!" But he hasn't taken more than five steps when he collapses of a heart attack. Not even the next moment is in our hands. Once we truly understand this, how can we be egoistic? As we breathe out, there is no guarantee that we will ever breathe in again. It is God's power that carries us through every moment. As we come to realize this, we will naturally feel humble, and we will begin to worship God. We will remember God at every step. But, combined with this attitude, we need to make an effort. Then, God's grace will flow to us and we will succeed in our efforts.

Question – It is said that hardships and suffering make us better human beings. Why, then, should we pray for the removal of our hardships and diseases?

Mother – You take medicine when you are sick, don't you? Even the mahatmas don't reject the use of medicines. When they get sick, they, too, do whatever is necessary to get well again. This shows the importance of self-effort. Indian culture has never taught us to sit idly, leaving everything to God. We should try to solve our problems and reduce our suffering. But our actions should be performed with an attitude of worship, without losing our humility, knowing that God is the power behind our every action. This is what the mahatmas and the scriptures teach us. For those who do spiritual practice with an understanding of these principles, and who have surrendered everything to God, there is no need for puja or prayers to relieve any of their illnesses, because they accept both happiness and sorrow as God's will. But for ordinary people, who do not have that measure of surrender, it is all right to seek relief through prayer and puja. Those who pray and perform puja will also gradually reach the state of selfless devotion.

We should do as much as lies within our capacity. If the difficulties nevertheless continue, let us accept them as God's will, as being for our own good. No matter what difficulties we have to face, we should always know that we are resting in God's lap. This attitude will give us the strength we need to overcome any adverse circumstances.

We see some people experiencing severe hardships during certain periods. There may be a long series of calamities. They may, for example, be blamed for something they didn't do, and even be sent to jail for crimes they didn't commit. There is the example of the son who met with an accident on his way to see his father, who was lying in a hospital. We hear of many such difficulties. In most of those people's lives, it is during certain periods that the difficulties occur. Whatever venture they undertake ends in failure. In some families, all the women become widows at a young age.

We should study these situations and try to understand them. The only explanation is that such tragedies are the results of actions done in the person's previous lives. They usually manifest during certain planetary periods or transitions. If people devote more time to worship and prayer during those periods, it will give them much solace. It will also give them the mental strength needed to overcome the obstacles they have to face.

The pujas performed in a Brahmasthanam Temple are not only rituals done to remove the difficulties caused by negative planetary influences; they are also a form of meditation. Moreover, through the satsangs that take place together with the pujas at such temples, the devotees learn about the spiritual principles. They are thus inspired to lead a dharmic life and to practice meditation. And as the rituals at the temples help to alleviate their problems, their faith and devotion grow.

Question – Is it necessary to worship images? Why do some religious texts oppose image worship?

Mother – We are not worshipping the image as such. Through the image, we worship God, who is all-pervading. The image symbolizes God; it is a means for us to make our minds one-pointed. We show our children pictures of a parrot and a mynah bird, and tell them, "That is a parrot and that is a mynah bird." This is necessary when the children are very young. Once they grow older, they no longer need those pictures to recognize the birds. Similarly, in the beginning, certain tools are necessary to help the minds of ordinary people focus on the Divine Consciousness. As one progresses in one's spiritual practice, the mind learns to become one-pointed without relying on such aids. Focusing on an image is a good way to train the mind to become one-pointed. Moreover, we cannot say that God is not present in the image. God pervades all living and non-living things. So God is also in the image. Image worship is a way of training people to see God in all sentient and insentient beings, and to cultivate an attitude of love and service toward the world.

Imagine that a man gives a present to the woman he loves. It may be something worth only five paise;[18] but to the woman who receives the gift, it is worth infinitely more than that. For, to her, it is imbued with her beloved.

We don't allow anyone to spit on the flag of our nation or political party, even though the cloth itself may be worth only a few rupees. A flag isn't just a piece of cloth, for once that cloth has been given the status of a flag, it represents a great ideal. We honor the flag because of our love and respect for the ideal it symbolizes. Similarly, it is God Himself that we see in the image we worship. The image serves as a mirror of the Divine Consciousness within us. We pray before the image with our eyes closed. The image helps us to turn our minds inward toward the indwelling God.

Even religions that oppose image worship do, in fact, worship images in one way or another. When a Christian

18 There are 100 paise in a rupee, which is the Indian currency.

worships the form of Jesus on the cross, or when a Muslim prays facing toward the Kaaba, those are also forms of image worship.

The negative side of image worship is that the worshipper may get attached to the image only, without understanding the principle behind it. But once people grasp the principle by listening to spiritual discourses and studying the scriptures, there is no problem.

We should try to provide an opportunity for spiritual education in our temples.

Question – Mother has many devotees from foreign countries. In general, Westerners appear to be more service-minded than we Indians are. What is the reason for this?

Mother – In western countries, organizations have been established for many different causes. When a crisis or disaster occurs, these organizations take responsibility for the care of those affected. The public lends its support to the organizations and participates in the service work. Also, the money that people donate is eligible for tax-deduction. This encourages people to come forward with financial donations for service activities. These charitable trusts play a large role in fostering in people the habit of giving. Long ago, the lives of Indians were rooted in dana (charity) and *yajna* (sacred offerings for the common good). Today, there are not enough facilities or programs available to teach people those ideals.

Question – Do heaven and hell really exist?

Mother – Heaven and hell exist here, within each of

us. It is our own actions that create either heaven or hell. When a person does something evil, he or she will have to accept the fruits thereof, that is for certain. That is what hell is.

Question – What are the ways to advance on the spiritual path?

Mother – First, we have to purify our character. If we pour milk into a dirty vessel, the milk will spoil. We have to clean the vessel before transferring milk into it. Those who desire to be spiritually uplifted should first try to purify themselves. To purify the mind is to eliminate negative and unnecessary thoughts and to reduce selfishness and desires. We have to make an effort to succeed in this. What we need more than anything is God's grace. And for God's grace to flow to us, we certainly have to be humble. Devotion and meditation prepare us for this.

Through meditation we attain not only peace of mind, but material prosperity as well. Meditation rooted in the understanding of the spiritual principles paves the way for enlightenment.

(*The following section is from an interview that the American documentary filmmaker Michael Tobias conducted with Mother*).

Question – Mother, what in your life appeared to you as the most miraculous?

Mother – Nothing has seemed especially miraculous to Mother. What is there to marvel about in external splendor? On the other hand, when we realize that everything is

God, each object and every moment of life becomes miraculous. What greater miracle is there than God?

Question – It is said that our love should express itself through our actions.

What can individuals do to put this into practice and propagate nonviolence and compassion?

Mother – We need to give up the notion that we are individuals, and act with the awareness that we are part of the Universal Consciousness. Only then can we put compassion and nonviolence fully into practice. You wonder if it is possible to do this. But even if we don't fully reach that state, shouldn't we at least strive as much as we can to love and to serve others, and keep that as our goal?

Question – What is Mother's reaction to the environmental problems of today?

Mother – The conservation of nature will be possible only when people fully recognize that they are a part of nature. The attitude that prevails today allows us to exploit nature indiscriminately. If we continue in this way, humanity itself will be destroyed. In the old days people prospered because they lived in harmony with nature.

The Puranas describe the earth as a cow that is milked for all necessities. When we milk a cow, we must make sure we leave enough milk for the calf before we take any milk for ourselves. The people of those times loved and protected the cow. They thought of her as their own mother. This was their attitude toward nature as a whole. What is needed today is that we begin to value Mother Nature as much as we value our own mother who gave birth to us.

When our mental outlook improves, the state of the environment will also improve. The ecological problems cannot be solved without a fundamental change in people's mental attitude.

Question – What is Mother's opinion about protecting fish and animals?

Mother – Humanity and nature are interdependent. People who live in areas unsuitable for cultivation, for example, on the coasts or in ice-bound regions, depend on fish for their food. And people have to fell trees to build houses and to make various articles. All this is necessary, but it should be done only according to people's needs. Today some animal, plant, and tree species are becoming extinct because of people's excessive greed. Many life forms that once existed on earth are now extinct. Those species perished because they couldn't withstand the changes that took place in nature. Nature loses her harmony when people exploit her. If we continue to exploit nature, it will lead to humanity's destruction, just as other species have become extinct.

Humankind is a part of nature and of all living beings on earth. We may take from nature what we need to survive, but we also have the responsibility to ensure that by taking from her bounty we do not destroy the rhythm and harmony of nature.

Suppose you pick a leaf from a jackfruit tree to make a spoon for eating kanji (rice gruel eaten by villagers in Kerala). But instead of taking just one leaf, you tear a whole branch from the tree. What would be the result? After you have made ten trips, the tree will have lost all its branches, and before long the whole tree will die. On the other hand, picking just a few leaves is a small loss that the tree can easily withstand. This should be our approach whenever we take anything from nature.

God has created each entity in nature in such a way that is useful to something else. A small fish is eaten by a large fish, and the large fish is hunted by an even larger fish. Nothing is wrong with humans taking just enough from nature to meet their needs. But taking from nature in excess is a form of himsa (violence), and this will lead to the downfall of humanity.

Question – How should we react to the social problems of today?

Mother – Today's problems are a matter of grave concern. It is essential that we learn the causes of those problems and deal with them. But change has to begin with the individual. When an individual changes for the better, the whole family benefits, and then society prospers. So, first, we ourselves should make an attempt to do good. When we change ourselves for the better, it influences everyone around us; it will bring about positive changes in them as well. We cannot change others by merely advising or scolding them. We have to set an example. We should be kind and loving toward everyone. Only through selfless love can we bring about a transformation in others. We may not see any immediate changes, but we should never lose hope or give up our efforts. At least our efforts will bring about a welcome change in us.

If we keep trying to straighten a dog's tail by putting the tail in a tube, the tail won't straighten, but our arm muscles will get stronger! Thus, when we make an effort with the aim of having an effect on others, we ourselves change for the better. But certain changes will definitely take place in others as well, even though we may not see it directly. And at least our attempts will help prevent society from deteriorating any further. It is through such efforts that we are able to maintain some degree of harmony in society.

A person swimming against a current may not move forward even an inch; but because of his efforts he will be able to stay where he is and not be swept away. If he gives up, he will drown. Similarly, it is essential to persevere in our efforts.

You may wonder, "What is the point of one person struggling alone in society, in a world so full of darkness?" Each of us has a candle, the candle of the mind. Light that candle with the flame of faith. Don't worry about how you will manage to cover such a great distance with such a small light. Just take one step at a time. You will discover that there is enough light to illumine each step along the way.

A man stood by the roadside feeling totally dejected. A passerby saw him and smiled at him. For this man who felt devoid of all hope, abandoned by all, that one smile had a tremendous effect. The very thought that there was someone who cared enough to look at him and smile gave him renewed energy. At that moment, he remembered a friend he hadn't seen for a long time, and he wrote him a letter. The friend was so happy to receive the letter that he gave ten rupees to a poor woman standing nearby. The woman went and bought a lottery ticket with the money. And, wonder of wonders, she won the lottery! While walking home with her prize money, she saw a sick beggar lying on the pavement. She thought, "It is thanks to God that I received this windfall. Let me use some of it to help this poor man." She took the beggar to a hospital and arranged for his treatment. When the beggar was released from the hospital, he happened to see an abandoned puppy that was cold and hungry and too weak to walk. The puppy whimpered piteously, and the beggar's heart melted. The beggar picked it up. He wrapped the puppy in a piece of cloth and lit a small fire by the roadside to warm it. He shared his food with the little dog, who after all that love and care, soon regained its strength. The puppy followed the beggar. That night, the beggar stopped in front of a house and asked if he could spend the night there. The family allowed the beggar and the little dog to sleep on their porch. During the night the beggar and the people of the house were awakened by the incessant barking of the puppy. They discovered that the house was on fire—right near the child's bedroom! At the very last moment they managed to rescue the child, and, working together, they put out the fire. So, one good turn led to another. Giving shelter to the beggar and his dog saved the family. The child grew up to be a saint. Countless people found joy and peace through their association with him.

If we analyze this, we will see that it all stemmed from one person's smile. That person didn't spend a single paise—all he did was smile at a man on the street. And that one smile affected the lives of many people. That one smile illumined people's lives.

Even the smallest things we do for others can bring about a great transformation in society. We may not be aware of it right away, but every good deed certainly bears fruit. We should therefore make sure that we perform our every action in a way that will benefit others. Even a smile has tremendous value. And a smile costs us nothing. Unfortunately, these days people often laugh just to ridicule others. That is not what we need. On the other hand, we should be able to laugh at our own faults and foibles.

No one is an isolated island. We are all joined to one another like the links of a chain. Whether we are aware of it or not, we influence others with our actions. The changes that take place in one individual will be reflected in other people.

It is pointless to say that we will try to improve only after all the others have improved. If we are willing to change, even though others are not, we will see corresponding changes taking place in society as well. Don't feel disheartened if you don't see a tangible result in yourself. The transformation is taking place internally. Any salutary change occurring in us will definitely bring about a transformation in society as well.

Question – Mother's smile seems to have a special quality. What is the reason for that?

Mother – Mother doesn't smile deliberately—it happens naturally. When you know the Self, there is only bliss. And a smile is, after all, a natural expression of that bliss. Does the moonlight on a full-moon night have to explain itself?

Question – But sometimes we see tears in your eyes, especially when you are comforting people. Is your natural bliss affected by external situations?

Mother – Mother's mind acts like a mirror. A mirror reflects whatever appears before it. When Mother's children weep, their sorrow reflects in Mother and tears come. Mother wants them to experience mental peace. Mother may appear to be grieving—but in Her inner Self, Mother feels no grief.

Speaking With a Group of Westerners

(A group of German devotees came to the ashram to receive Mother's *darshan. Most of them had been doing spiritual practice for years. The following is their conversation with* Mother.*)*

Question – How long should the interval be between a meal and meditation?

Mother – My children, don't meditate immediately after a meal. Wait for at least two hours after a main meal. If you've eaten only a light meal, let half an hour pass before starting to meditate. When you sit for meditation, your mind goes to the part of the body on which you are trying to concentrate. As the meditator concentrates on his heart or on the spot between the eyebrows, much of his energy flows toward the point of concentration, leaving insufficient power for digestion to take place. Indigestion could therefore occur, with discomforts such as vomiting and headaches. So, begin your meditation only after allowing enough time for proper digestion to take place.

Question – How should we repeat our mantras?

Mother – When you repeat your mantra, concentrate either on the form of your Beloved Deity[19] or on the sound of the mantra. It is good to visualize each letter (syllable) of the mantra in your mind as you chant. You can focus the mind on the sound produced as you chant. It is in controlling our thoughts that repeating the mantra is most useful. The mantra is the oar we use to row to the Supreme Being.

Today, your mind is attached to diversity. Repeating a mantra will help you to free the mind from all that diversity and to center it on God. Mother has seen many people worry because they cannot visualize their Beloved Deity as they chant. If you cannot see the Deity, it is enough to remember His or Her name, and continue to repeat the mantra. Concentrate either on the letters or on the sound. During meditation, if you can focus your mind on the form, that is enough; it isn't necessary to chant the mantra at that time. But the chanting should go on in your mind continuously, when you are working, walking, sitting, traveling, or doing anything at all. In this way, the mind will always rest in God in a subtle way. Don't worry if you don't get full concentration. At least you can pay attention to the sound of the mantra.

Each time you chant, you can imagine that you are offering a flower at the feet of your Beloved Deity. Keeping your eyes closed, pick a flower from your heart, bring it to the feet of your Beloved Deity and place it there. If that isn't possible, concentrate on the sound of the mantra or on the visualized forms of the letters of the mantra. Whichever method you choose, don't let the mind wander; keep it tied to your Beloved Deity.

19 When Mother refers to the Beloved Deity, She means whatever aspect of the Divine is God to us; for example the Divine Mother, Krishna, or Christ.

Question – Is it necessary to repeat the mantra during meditation?

Mother – No, that isn't necessary if you are able to fix your mind on the form.

Question – How do we focus the mind on the form of our Beloved Deity as we meditate?

Mother – Visualize the form of your Beloved Deity repeatedly from head to foot and from foot to head. You can imagine that you are circumambulating the Deity, or running around and frolicking with Him or Her. Or that the Deity gets away from you and that you are running, trying to catch up with Him or Her. You can imagine that you are sitting in the Deity's lap and are giving Him or Her a kiss, or that you are combing the Deity's hair, or that the Deity is combing and smoothing your hair. All these visualizations are meant to keep the mind bound to your Beloved Deity.

As you visualize the divine form, pray, for example, "O Mother, lead me!" "O Father, lead me!" "Eternal Light, lead me!" or "Ocean of Compassion, lead me!"

Think of how far the mind travels in a second! These visualizations are done to stop the mind from going anywhere. You may not see any of this in Vedanta, but only through taking these steps can you bring what Vedanta talks about to the level of your own experience.

Question – How can we chant the mantra or remember the form of our Beloved Deity while we work? Won't we forget to chant?

Mother – Imagine that your brother is lying in the

hospital in critical condition. Will you be able to stop thinking about him even when you are at work? You will think about him constantly, whatever you are busy with. "Has he regained consciousness? Is he talking? Is he feeling better? When can he come home?" Nothing but your brother will be on your mind. But you will still be able to do your work. In the same way, if we think of God as our closest relative, as our very own, it won't be difficult for us to remember God and to chant the mantra.

Question – Will all the brahmacharis and brahmacharinis residing here attain realization?

Mother – The children who have come here have come for two different reasons. There are those who make the decision to come because they have developed total detachment toward the things of the world, and then there are those who are imitating that group and come here out of an initial fervor. But if they make the effort, they, too, can absorb this spiritual samskara and make progress. Haven't even some of those who were living in evil ways come to the right path through satsang (association with great souls)? Valmiki was a forest dweller who robbed and murdered people. Through satsang and his subsequent effort, he became a great sage and our first poet. Satsang also had a great effect on Prahlada, who became the foremost of devotees, despite being born from a lineage of asuras (demons).[20]

20 When the demon king Hiranyakasipu's wife was pregnant, the devas (celestial beings) attacked the asuras (demons). Hiranyakasipu was performing severe austerities at that time. The devas wanted to destroy the child that Kayadhu carried in her womb. They were worried that the child would become a threat to them in future. But when Devendra was kidnapping Kayadhu, Sage Narada intervened and stopped him. Narada knew that the child about to be born was destined to be his disciple and would become famous as a great devotee of Lord Vishnu. So Narada

Even if some people come here because of nothing more than an initial fervor, they can truly change if they try to grasp the teachings, assimilate them, and apply them to their lives. Isn't it possible to learn all about a craft by constantly associating with a person who is a master of that craft? But without staying close to the adept and observing him or her, you won't learn anything. Similarly, by being here at the ashram and taking part in ashram life, a person can progress in due course, and a spiritual disposition will be created within him or her. If there is no change in a person even after a long period of association, then we will just have to accept that it is the result of that person's karma from previous lives. It is pointless to blame anyone.

In a certain village, a *sannyasi* sat under a peepul tree every day, meditating and repeating a mantra. The villagers brought him fruits and pastries and offered their services. A young man who observed this day after day started thinking that surely life would be free from problems if he were to become a monk like that. So, he went to a nearby village, donned the ochre robe of a sannyasi, sat down under a tree and started meditating and repeating a mantra. Soon people began arriving to offer their respects to the sannyasi. Fruits and sweet dishes arrived in plenty. There were many beautiful women among those who came to see the young man. After a few days he disappeared. He had taken off with one of the women.

---

brought Kayadhu to his hermitage, and there he gave her discourses every day about Lord Vishnu and the wonderful stories relating to Him. And the child in the womb imbibed everything earnestly. Even when Kayadhu fell asleep due to exhaustion, the child in the womb responded to the saint's stories! So while in the womb, Prahlada was exposed to stories of the divine incarnations of the Lord. He also spent most of his childhood at Narada's ashram.

Those who come here only to play a game of pretense won't get away with it. Only those who have total faith and surrender will attain the ultimate state. The others will eventually go their way. Why worry about them? This is a battlefield. If you can succeed here, you can conquer the whole world—the whole universe will be under your control.

Question – If God is the cause of everything, isn't He also the cause of the numerous illnesses we see today?

Mother – God is the cause of everything, He has also told us how to lead our lives. He speaks to us through the mahatmas. What is the use of blaming God for the hardships we experience when we do not obey His teachings?

A health tonic helps you to get better, but if you drink the whole bottle in one gulp, without listening to the doctor's instructions on how it should be taken, whatever health you still have could be ruined. And if you don't tune a radio properly, it will only cause a disturbance. When you tune it in the right way, the music will give you a sense of pleasure and satisfaction. Similarly, people suffer because they fail to grasp the most important points in life. It is by grasping the key points in life that we can find happiness, and those principles can be learned through satsang. Listening to spiritual discourses can help us remove many problems. But if you live close to a spiritual master who abides in the ultimate Truth, and follow his or her instruction, your life will be ever joyful; you will never have to fall into danger. The life of those who neither learn about the true principles of life through books or spiritual discourses, nor experience the presence of a spiritual master, will surely take a downward turn.

Many of the illnesses we see today are the result of the selfish actions of humanity. We eat food that is toxic and adulterated. The pesticides and fertilizers used to cultivate grains and vegetables are toxic enough to kill people if they inhale them. We eat crops produced in this way and adulterated for excessive profit. How can our health not be affected? The use of alcohol and drugs is also the cause of many illnesses. But people aren't even given pure medicines to treat those illnesses, for the medicines are also adulterated. Thus, the inhuman behavior of humans is the reason why illnesses are multiplying to such an extent at present. We cannot blame God for this. God doesn't make anyone sick. Nor does God make anyone suffer. There are no imperfections in God's creation. Humans are the ones who distort everything. We should live according to God's will, in harmony with nature. Then most of today's illnesses can be eliminated.

Question – Today not even children are free from illness. What mistakes did they commit?

Mother – Their parents are often inadvertently the cause of their illnesses. After all, the children are born from the seeds of parents who live on poisonous food. How, then, can they be healthy? Even cow's milk contains toxic substances nowadays. Cows eat grass and other types of fodder that have been sprayed with pesticides.

The children of alcoholics and drug addicts won't be healthy. They may also have deformities because the semen of their fathers may not have had the factors needed to engender a healthy body. The children of those who take an excessive amount of allopathic drugs are also prone to illnesses. It is because of the negative actions those souls have committed in their previous lives that they have now had to be reborn as children of such parents. Thus, they have to suffer the consequences of the negative actions of their parents as well. Our happiness and sorrow all depend on our actions. The root cause of everything lies in karma. If we perform our actions with great care and alertness, we won't have to experience suffering. We will be able to enjoy happiness always.

People cause their own difficulties. They experience the fruits not of mistakes they haven't committed, but of those they have committed. Today people do not live as part of God's creation; they live in their own creation and experience the results thereof. So we cannot blame God and say it is His fault. As long as we follow God's path we won't have to be sorry; we won't even know what suffering is.

Question – The scriptures talk about reincarnation. On what basis does an individual soul get a new body?

Mother – Each individual soul is given a new birth in accordance with its prior samskara (level of internal refinement). It is due to the samskara attained in its previous life that the individual soul gets a human birth. If a person performs good actions and leads a pure life, he or she can verily become God. But if a person persists in living like an animal, despite being born as a human, he or she will have to be born again in a lower life form.

There is an aura surrounding our bodies. Just as we record music and conversations on tape, the aura records each of our thoughts and actions. The aura's recording has different parts for different actions: good deeds are captured by the aura above the waist, and bad actions by the lower part. If a person has done mainly good deeds, he or she ascends to a higher level after death. The soul reaches the world of the ancestors or is born again in accordance with the limits set by his or her actions. But if a person has committed predominantly evil actions, the aura of that soul falls to the ground and turns into food for worms and insects, and the soul will be born again as a bird or an animal.

When a good egg hatches, a bird will emerge. If the egg is bad, there won't be any bird. The broken egg rots on the ground and gets eaten by worms and insects.

Living only for today's happiness will lead only to tomorrow's sorrow.

If you spit upwards while lying on your back because you are too lazy to get up, the spit will land on your own body. Similarly, for every action, there will be a corresponding reaction from nature. That is certain.

Question – If we have performed various actions in our previous lives, why are we not aware of them now?

Mother – Can you remember all the things you did when you were a small child? We can't even recall all the things we've done in this life! A song you memorized yesterday may be forgotten today. How, then, can you expect to remember what happened in a previous life? But when your mind becomes subtle through spiritual practice, you will know everything. When we talk about the fruits of actions done in previous lives, the fruits of our actions done unknowingly in this life are included as well.

The happiness and sorrow we experience now are the results of our previous actions, either from previous lives or from this life itself. If we use our intelligence and act properly, we can live contentedly. We can become the children of bliss.

Question – When our foot happens to touch someone, we are supposed to touch that person with our hand and then bring the hand to our forehead. Isn't all that superstition?

Mother – Those practices were instituted by our ancestors to cultivate good habits in people. We say to a child, "Telling a lie will make you blind." If this were true, how many people would be able to see today? But by saying this, we are able to correct the child's habit of telling lies. When we touch someone with our foot, we are asked to touch that person and show reverence. This is meant to cultivate humility in us. A person who practices this will not think of kicking someone even in anger.

There is another reason for this practice. There is a connection between our feet and our head. When the foot hits something, certain nerves in the head are affected. When we bow down, the tension in those nerves is relieved.

But mainly, these practices help us to develop good conduct.

Question – Mother, can life be divided into two aspects, the spiritual and the material? Which one gives us happiness?

Mother – My children, there is no need to see the spiritual and material sides of life as separate. That difference exists only in the attitude of the mind. We need to understand spirituality and live accordingly. Only then will life become blissful. Spirituality teaches us how to live a life of true happiness. Say that the material side of life is rice, and the spiritual side is sugar. Spirituality is the sugar that sweetens the rice pudding. An understanding of spirituality is what makes life sweet.

If you rely on the materialistic side of life, there will be suffering. Those who desire only worldly pleasures must be prepared to experience suffering as well. Only those who are prepared to suffer for it should pray for worldly needs. The worldly side will constantly pester and torment us. This doesn't mean that you should completely renounce worldly life. Mother is saying only that you should have an understanding of spirituality while you are living in the world. Then you will not be weakened by suffering. In this world, no one who claims to be our own, our kith or kin, really belongs to us. No one who claims to be our family is our real family. Only God is our true family. Anyone else could turn against us at any moment. People love us only because of a desire for their own happiness. When sickness, sorrow, or hardship comes, we have to bear it alone. So let us be attached to God alone. If we are attached to the world, it will be difficult for us to regain our freedom. How many countless lives a person has to live to be liberated from attachments!

Life should be lived as if we were performing a duty. Then we won't succumb to sadness if others turn against us or forsake us. If someone we have loved more than our own life suddenly turns against us, we won't go to pieces.

There will be no reason for us to despair.

If there is a cut on your hand, it won't heal if you just sit and cry. Nor will it help if you cry when you lose your wealth or your kith and kin. Crying will not bring them back. But if we can understand and accept the fact that those who are with us today could leave us tomorrow, we can live happily, free from sorrow, no matter who may turn against us or leave us. This doesn't mean that we shouldn't love anyone. On the contrary, we should love everyone. But our love should be selfless. We should love without any expectations. This will help us to avoid sorrow.

Worldly life contains sorrow. Yet, life can still give us happiness if we have some understanding of spirituality. If we jump into a rough sea without having had any training, we could be overwhelmed by the waves and even drown. But those who know how to swim in the sea can easily handle even big waves. Similarly, if we allow spirituality to be the foundation of our lives, we can go forward without faltering under any circumstances, no matter how difficult. The mind finds happiness in one object and hates another. Some people feel they can't live without cigarettes, while others are disturbed by cigarette smoke. Happiness and sorrow reside in the mind. If you control your mind and direct it toward the right path, there will be only happiness in your life. For this you need spiritual knowledge; and if you live in accordance with that knowledge, there can be no sorrow.

Try to chant a mantra always. Talk only about God. Relinquish all selfishness. Surrender everything to God. If we can live in this way, we won't experience suffering.

If we can so easily become attached to anything in the

world, why can't we become attached to God? Our tongues know how to talk about everything; why can't we teach our tongues to chant our mantra? If we can do this, not only we ourselves, but also those around us, will find peace.

Most people talk about their problems with everyone around them. This doesn't remove their problems; it only makes those who have to listen to them unhappy as well. It is like a small snake that tries to swallow a big snake.

To be worldly is to forget God; it is to want nothing but your own happiness, relying on material objects for that purpose, and being forced to suffer most of your life for the sake of little fragments of pleasure. This is how people lose their peace of mind; and those around them are also affected. To be selfless and surrender everything to God, knowing that everything really belongs to God—that is spirituality. Those who live in this way not only experience inner peace themselves, but also engender peace in the hearts of those around them.

Question – Mother, you have said that our devotion shouldn't be prompted by desires, but that it should be rooted in our understanding of spiritual principles. What is the reason for this?

Mother – Real progress can be made only through devotion rooted in the essential principles. We should learn to lead our lives along the right path. Devotion teaches us how to do this. There is only bliss in a real devotee's life. But if your devotion isn't accompanied by an understanding of the spiritual principles, your entire life will be out of tune. Such a life won't give you any happiness. This is why Mother says that when you worship God you should have an understanding of the spiritual principles, and you should pray for true devotion.

Today the prayers of most people are driven entirely by desires. Their devotion isn't based on any real understanding. They go to the temple when they want something, and make a vow to give God something in return if they get what they want. This cannot be called devotion. Happiness cannot be attained in that way. They love God if they accomplish their objective, and hate God if they fail. Their life is one of broken, intermittent faith.

In a village there were two couples who had been married for ten years. Neither couple had any children. One couple felt so sad about this that they started praying to God. They prayed every day for a child. Then one night the husband had a dream. A divine being appeared to him and asked, "If you are given a child, will you feel satisfied?" He replied, "Without a child, I will never be happy. If only I had a child, I would always be contented." The divine being blessed him and disappeared. Soon after, his wife became pregnant. They both were overjoyed. But their happiness didn't last long, for they worried about the child to be born. Their constant thoughts were "Will the baby's limbs and organs be intact? Will our child be healthy? Will he be handsome?" Earlier they had prayed to God out of their desire to have a child, but now they didn't have a spare moment to think of God. Their thoughts were only on the child about to be born. They didn't experience a moment of peace.

The baby arrived. It was a healthy boy and the parents were very happy. They began saving money for their son's education. As the boy grew older he started school. Each morning, when the boy set off for school, the parents would worry about him. Would anyone hurt him? What if he fell somewhere? They couldn't relax until their son returned home. As the child grew up, he became obstinate and mischievous. He refused to obey his parents and paid no attention to his lessons. Now the mother's and father's only concerns were for their son's future. But as the boy grew older, his bad habits intensified. Everyone complained about his behavior. When the boy reached college, he started drinking. He was constantly pestering his parents for money. This became a daily habit. He didn't hesitate to verbally abuse and even beat them. The parents now feared the time each day when he returned home. The son sold his parents' belongings, one by one. One day when they refused to give him any money, he threatened them with a knife. Fearing for their lives, they borrowed money for everything he wanted, as all they had owned was now lost. When they were unable to pay their debts, the local people turned against them and stopped lending them any money. Finally, when his parents were no longer of any use to him, he left them and they never saw him again. They had lived only for their son, and now he was gone; their neighbors hated them and they had lost everything. They could only weep. There was nothing but despair left in their lives.

If it is only worldly happiness we want, we should also be prepared to bear the sorrows that come with it.

The other couple had also prayed to God, but not for a child. They prayed for God alone. Their devotion was based on true love for God. The fact that they didn't have a child never bothered them. Their prayer was: "We have no children. Therefore, God, make us look upon everyone as Your child!" We will have children if it is God's will. Why worry about it? Devotion for God is what we should pray for. That was this couple's attitude. They had a real understanding of spirituality. They were aware of that which is eternal and of the purpose of life. They chanted their mantras constantly, and during their spare time they joyfully recounted stories about God and sang devotional songs with their friends and family. Each day they prayed that they would be able to love and serve everyone. They also gave a portion of their income to the poor. God was pleased with their selfless devotion. And even though they didn't pray for it, they were blessed with a son. Their devotion continued unabated after the child was born. Although grateful and happy, they didn't feel excessive joy at the birth of their son. They continued to lead a life that was dedicated to God. They told their son spiritual stories and taught him to pray and sing devotional songs at a young age. Consequently, the boy became good-natured and was dear to everyone. The parents were very loving toward their child but weren't excessively attached to him. They held fast to God. As they approached old age, they didn't expect companionship from anyone. God was the center of their lives. But many people came to the couple and served them with reverence and love, for they were attracted to the couple's innocent devotion and their selfless love for all.

Because of their selflessness, they enjoyed a happy life. They were joyful both before and after the birth of their son. And because they prayed, "God, make us see everyone as Your child," they were given much more than a son; they were given many people who loved them and served them.

Both couples had bhakti (devotion), but one couple's devotion was kamya bhakti (devotion driven by desire), while the other couple's bhakti was unmotivated devotion—love for love's sake alone.

To the first couple, their son was everything. They thought he would be with them forever. To them, God was no more than a tool to fulfill their desires. As soon as they got what they wanted, they forgot about God. And when their son left them, they were overcome with despair.

But the second couple understood that only God is true and eternal in this illusory world. They knew that no one loves anyone above his or her own happiness. They also knew that neither a child, a spouse, wealth, nor anything else would come with them at the time of death. Therefore, their only goal was to realize the Self, which alone is everlasting. And they lived in tune with that goal. The devotion that they and their family had was rooted in tattva (the true spiritual principle). They did not grieve if anyone turned against them. They loved even those who resented them. Because they had surrendered their lives to God, they were happy.

My children, devotion should be based only on our desire for God. Then God will give us everything; there will be no need to worry about who will look after us in our old age. No sincere devotees have ever died of starvation or suffered because they lacked someone to look after them. And why think about what happens to the body after death? The body will start stinking shortly after death. It will be buried or cremated. There is no need to waste your life worrying about such things.

Why be anxious thinking about tomorrow? What happened even a moment ago is like a cancelled check. There is no point in losing your strength thinking about it. Live today with great care and alertness, and tomorrow will be your friend.

Devotion is important. But to pray and then to talk badly about others is not devotion. Those with devotion do not harbor jealousy or ill will toward others. We should try to see everyone as God—that is devotion. Doing good deeds with great attention is also devotion. What Mother calls devotion is the ability to discriminate between the eternal and the ephemeral. This is what is needed.

Question – Is it not God who makes us do both what is right and what is wrong?

Mother – That is true if you really have the awareness that God makes you do everything. In that case, when you experience the benefit from a good deed or the punishment from a negative action, you should equally be able to think, "It is God who gives everything."

God is not responsible for our mistakes. We ourselves are. Blaming God for the problems that arise out of our ignorance is like blaming the petrol when our car hits something due to our careless driving. God has made it clear how we should live in this world. We cannot blame God for the consequences of not following His instructions.

Question – In the Bhagavad Gita it is said that we should perform our actions without any desire for their fruits. How can we work without wanting the fruits of our work?

Mother – The Lord said this to enable us to live a life

free from suffering. Do your actions with great care and attention, and without being consumed by anxiety regarding the results. The appropriate results will come of their own accord. If you study, do it with attention. There is no need to worry about whether or not you will pass. If you are building a house, build it carefully according to the plans, without tormenting yourself wondering if the building will stand. Do good deeds, and good results are bound to follow. If you sell rice of good quality, without any stones in it, everyone will buy it. That is the desired fruit of your efforts in selecting good grains, and then parboiling, drying, and husking the rice. But if you adulterate the rice in order to make more profit, you will receive the punishment for that, either today or tomorrow. You will also lose your peace of mind. So perform your actions with care and attention, with the attitude that everything you do is an offering to God. You will get the fruits of what you do in just measure, neither more nor less, whether you worry about the results beforehand or not. So why waste time thinking about it? Wouldn't it be better to use that energy to do the action really well instead? Or, wouldn't it be better to focus your mind on God instead of wasting that time?

Question – If the Self is all-pervading, shouldn't it be present in the body even after death? Then why does death take place?

Mother – Just because a light bulb burns out, it doesn't mean that there is no electric power. If you switch off a fan, you won't feel any air flow, but the air doesn't disappear. Or, say that you blow air into a balloon, tie it, and send it up into the sky. If the balloon breaks, the air doesn't cease to exist—it is still there. Similarly, the Self is present everywhere. God is everywhere. Death occurs not because of the absence of the Self but because of the failure of the upadhi (the support or instrument) (i.e. the body). Death is the destruction of the upadhi; it has nothing to do with any deficiency in the Self.

Question – Is it possible to attain the state of Self-realization through spiritual practice, reading books, and listening to discourses only, without the aid of a spiritual master?

Mother – You won't become a mechanic by just learning about it from books. You have to train with an experienced mechanic. You need to watch what that person is doing and learn from it. Similarly, to be aware of the obstacles that may arise during spiritual practice and to overcome them in order to reach the goal, you need a spiritual master.

The directions on how to take a medicine are written on the label. But you still shouldn't take the medicine without first consulting a doctor. The label gives you only general directions. The doctor decides how the medicine should be used, taking into account the health and constitution of each patient. If you don't follow the doctor's directions, the medicine could do more harm than good. Similarly, you may be able to learn about spirituality and spiritual practice by reading books and listening to discourses; but to overcome certain difficulties that may arise, and to reach the goal through spiritual practice, you need a spiritual master.

When a seedling is transplanted from one place to another, some soil from the original place should be brought with it, for then it won't be so difficult for the plant to take root and adapt to its new home. Without a little of the original soil, it will be difficult for the plant to get used to the new soil. The presence of a spiritual master is like the soil from the original site.

In the beginning it is very difficult for a seeker to persevere in his or her spiritual practice. The master's presence gives the disciple the strength needed to transcend all the obstacles and remain firmly rooted in spiritual life. An apple tree needs a special climate to grow properly. It also needs water and fertilizers at certain times. Any pests that infest the tree have to be destroyed. Similarly, the master creates circumstances suitable for the disciple's spiritual practice, and protects him or her from all obstacles.

The master indicates what form of spiritual practice you should do. He or she decides which spiritual path you should follow and whether your spiritual practice should be the practice of discrimination (between the eternal and the transitory), selfless service, yoga, a certain type of meditation, or mantra chanting and prayer. Some people do not have the physical constitution needed to do yoga, and there are those who shouldn't meditate for long stretches at a time. What would happen if you were to let 125 people board a bus that is meant to fit only 25? You can't operate a small blender in the same way as you would run a large grinder; if you run it continuously for a long time, it will overheat and get damaged. The master suggests the appropriate spiritual practice according to each person's physical, mental, and intellectual state.

The master knows the nature of your mind and body better than you do. He or she instructs you according to your qualifications. If you ignore this and start doing spiritual practice according to some information you've obtained from somewhere, without receiving the proper guidance, you could become mentally unbalanced. If a person meditates excessively, the head may become too hot. He or she may then lose sleep. The master gives instructions according to the nature of each individual, as to which part of the body to focus on during meditation—for example, the heart or the spot between the eyebrows—and for how long to meditate.

When you embark on a journey, if you are accompanied by a person who lives where you are heading and who knows all the routes leading there, you will reach your destination quickly. Otherwise a journey that should take only an hour may take ten. Even if you have a map, you could still lose your way in the unfamiliar terrain. You could end up in a dangerous area. But there is nothing to fear if you have a companion who knows the way. The spiritual master's role can be compared to that of such a guide. The master is thoroughly familiar with all the different paths on the spiritual journey. There may be obstacles at any step of your spiritual practice, and without a master to guide you it will be difficult for you to maintain your spiritual practice when obstacles arise.

If you receive initiation from a satguru, you can progress very rapidly. You cannot make yogurt by just adding milk to milk; you have to add a little yogurt to the milk. Mantra initiation given by a satguru is similar to this. It awakens the seeker's spiritual power.

Question – Is it not slavery to obey a spiritual master?

Mother – It is difficult to get rid of the ego through spiritual practice alone. To remove the ego, you have to practice certain steps prescribed by a qualified master. When we bow our heads before a spiritual master, we are not focusing on that individual, but on the principles that the master embodies. We are bowing down to that ideal, so that we may also reach that level. Only through humility can we ascend. There is a tree within every seed. But if a seed remains in the storeroom claiming to be a tree, it will just turn into fodder for a mouse! The real nature of the seed emerges after it bows down and goes beneath the soil.

The umbrella unfolds when the button is pressed down. It can then protect people from the rain and the sun.

When, as children, we obeyed, respected, and honored our parents, teachers, and elders, we developed; we grew wiser and cultivated positive qualities and habits. Similarly, through the disciple's obedience to the master, he or she rises to an expansive state of consciousness, and becomes the king of kings.

The true master is the very embodiment of renunciation. We come to understand what truth, dharma, selflessness, and love are because the master lives those qualities. The master is the life of those qualities. By obeying and emulating the satguru, we cultivate those qualities in ourselves.

When we have boarded a plane, the crew members ask us to fasten our seatbelts. They don't do this to show their superiority, but only to ensure our safety. Similarly, when the master instructs the disciple to practice self-control and restraint and to obey certain rules, it is for the development of the disciple. The master instructs the disciple in order to protect him or her from any difficulties that may arise. The master knows that the downward plunges the disciple may take due to the ego could land not only the disciple but others in danger as well.

People obey the hand signals of the traffic police. This helps to avoid countless accidents. The satguru saves the disciple from situations that could lead to spiritual ruin due to the disciple's sense of "I" and "mine." The master gives the disciple the training he or she needs in order to avoid such situations in the future.

Obedience to a spiritual master is not slavery—far from it. The master's sole aim is the disciple's safety and ultimate freedom. The master is someone who can truly show us the way. A real master will never think of the disciple as a slave. The master feels only unbounded love toward the disciple. The master's wish is to see the disciple succeed, even if the master out of his or her own resolve has to accept defeat in some way in the process. A perfect master is a true mother.

Question – Do those who depend on God in their lives have to make an effort?

Mother – My children, without effort you cannot succeed in life. To just sit there without making any effort, claiming that God will take care of everything is sheer laziness. Such people say that God will look after everything, and yet they do not surrender fully to that. Whenever any work is required, they claim that God will take care of everything. But as soon as they feel hungry, they make the effort to fill their bellies, even if it means they have to steal to get some food. They don't wait patiently for God to bring them food! When it comes to hunger and other personal matters, their surrender to God is only words.

God cares about every aspect of our lives. This doesn't mean that we will achieve any results by sitting with our arms crossed when the occasion really calls for action. God hasn't given us life, health, and an intellect for us to waste our lives being lazy! We should be willing to work according to God's instructions.

Fire can be used to burn the house down as well as to cook food. Similarly, if we don't utilize what God has given us in its intended way, it could do more harm than good. Whenever your effort is required, act accordingly, as an offering to God. Only then will you get the most appropriate results.

A disciple went out begging for food. He was out all day but didn't get anything. He returned to the master that evening, tired and hungry. He felt angry with God because he hadn't received any alms. He said to the master, "From now on, I don't want to depend on God. You always tell us that we will get everything we want if we surrender to God. Why should I take refuge in a God who can't give me even one meal? It was a mistake to put my trust in God!"

The master said to him, "I will give you 100,000 rupees. Will you give me your eyes in return?"

The disciple replied, "I would be blind without my eyes! Who would sell their eyes for any price?"

"Forget the eyes then. Will you give me your tongue?"

"How would I be able to speak without my tongue?"

"Give me your arm then. Or, if that isn't possible, your leg will do. I'll give you 100,000 rupees!'

"My body is more valuable than money. No one would want to lose any part of their body."

Perceiving the attitude of the disciple, the master said, "Your body is indeed invaluable. But God gave it to you without taking anything in return. Still you criticize God. God didn't give you that priceless body so that you would just sit idly. You are meant to live a life of action, with great attention and awareness."

Three men were each given some seeds. The first man locked his seeds away safely in a box. The second man ate his seeds straight away to quell his hunger. The third man planted his seeds, watered, and cultivated them.

Those who sit around doing nothing, claiming that God will look after everything are like the man who keeps his seeds in a box. Those seeds are of no use to anyone. Such people are simply lazy. They are a burden to the world. They don't utilize their instruments, i.e., the body, mind, and intellect, given to them by God.

The man who ate his seeds was able to satisfy his hunger temporarily. This is what worldly beings are like. Their goal is temporary happiness. But the man who understood how to utilize his seeds in the proper way, who planted and cultivated them, was able to feed himself and his family with the fruits he got as a result. And he could plant more seeds from those fruits, providing his neighbors with what they needed as well. Similarly, only by understanding the real, intended use of the instruments we have been given by God, and utilizing them in the proper way, can we live useful lives and reach the true goal.

My children, to surrender to God is to use this instrument God has given us, and to do so with the proper care and attention. Sitting idly without making the slightest effort is a great sin against God.

What did Lord Krishna say in the Gita? He said, "Arjuna, you should fight, remembering Me!" He didn't say, "You don't have to do anything. Just sit there and I will protect you." If we take one step toward God, God will take a hundred steps toward us. But we usually don't have the surrender needed to take that one step.

My children, do not forget it is God who gives us the ability and the circumstances needed to make an effort. But the success of our effort also depends on God's grace. It is therefore our duty to make an effort, surrendering the fruits, whatever they may be, to God.

We should be like a piece of wood in God's hands. At different times God may cut us into pieces, make a toy out of us, or use us as fuel for a fire. Our surrender to God should be such that we can say, "Let God do whatever He wants. I will happily accept anything." When we have this attitude what we do becomes right action. Then, neither victory nor defeat will affect us. We experience inner peace and contentment.

My children, we should try to disseminate spiritual principles to others by putting those principles into practice in our own lives. We cannot spread this knowledge among the people through talk alone. The time people waste through talking would be enough to put the teachings into practice! Ordinary people like to emulate the deeds of those who enjoy status and position in society. That is why it is so important that those who enjoy a high position should try to be positive role models for others to follow.

A government minister once visited a village, which happened to be the dirtiest village in the whole country. He spent a night as the guest of the mayor of the place. There were piles of garbage everywhere along the roads, and the open drains overflowed with filthy, stagnant waste water. The whole area was permeated with a terrible stench.

The minister asked the mayor why the place was so dirty. The mayor said, "The people here are ignorant. They don't know anything about cleanliness. They simply don't care. I've tried to teach them, but they won't listen. I've told them to clean the village, but they won't do it. So, I've given up." The mayor went on and on, blaming the villagers. The minister listened patiently without saying anything. They had dinner and then the minister went to bed.

When the mayor got up the next morning he couldn't find the minister. He searched throughout the house, but there was no sign of him. He asked the servants, but no one had seen the minister. The mayor was alarmed. He left the house and went out looking for the minister. At last he found him. The minister was out on the road, cleaning up the rubbish all by himself. He was heaping garbage into a big pile and setting it on fire. When he saw this, the mayor felt ashamed. He said to himself, "How can I stand here doing nothing, when the minister himself is working like this?" So he joined him and started cleaning up the village. When the villagers came out into the streets, they were surprised to see the two men doing such dirty work. They felt that they couldn't just stand there and watch while the minister and the mayor cleaned the village. So they joined in the work. In no time the whole village was spotlessly clean. All the rubbish had been removed and the drains were clear. There was not a speck of rubbish to be seen. The whole village looked completely different.

My children, it usually takes less time to demonstrate something through action than to really get it across with words. We should be willing to take action, without waiting to see whether or not anyone will be there to help us. Then, people are bound to join in and help. If we just stand aside blaming and criticizing others, we do that from our own polluted minds, and their minds will then become polluted like ours. So, my children, we need to take action, and not just talk. Change is possible only through action.

Question – It is said that we should be even minded when receiving either praise or blame. But it is also said that the Lord (Vishnu) was pleased when the celestial beings sang in praise of Him. Wasn't the Lord influenced by the praise, then?

Mother – The Lord is never flattered by praise. He is equanimity itself. Praise and abuse are the same to Him. Even if you were to throw dog excreta at the Lord, He would give you ice cream in return. Such is His mind. That is equanimity.

The Lord taught the devas (celestial beings) a lesson. To make them suffer a little at first, He kept His eyes closed for awhile after they arrived. Though they called out many times, He didn't show the slightest sign of being aware of them. Finally, they prayed to him with aching hearts. Only then did he open His eyes. As a result of their prayers, they were able to see Him in their hearts as well. Those mantras were not uttered to praise Him or to get what they wanted; they were the prayers uttered by devotees as they beheld the Lord. They prayed for a revelation of the true nature of the Self. And the Lord was pleased with the innocent hearts of His devotees. It is impossible to please the Lord if it doesn't come from the heart.

Question – How does a mahatma view the world?

Mother – A woman in love goes to see a play in which her lover is acting. As she watches the play, she enjoys his acting. She sees that character through him. But it is always her beloved she sees behind the role being played, and this is why she enjoys the play. She is delighted by it. Similarly, everything a mahatma sees in the world is simply a different role being played by God. The mahatmas see God behind the world and behind every individual.

Question – Can we change destiny through our own effort?

Mother – If you perform your actions as an offering to God, you can transcend destiny. Avoid laziness at all costs, and do your best without blaming destiny. A person who refuses to make any effort in life and then blames fate is simply lazy.

Two friends had their horoscopes done. It turned out that they were both destined to die from a snakebite. From that day on, one of them was overwhelmed with anxiety, thinking constantly about snakes and death. He became mentally ill, and thus his family also lost their peace of mind. But his friend, who had been given the same prediction, refused to yield to any negative thoughts. Instead, he looked for a solution. He searched for ways to avoid being bitten by a snake. When he understood that he could do only so much, he took refuge in God. But he still decided to use the intelligence and health given to him by God, and he stayed in his room taking all the precautions necessary to prevent his fate. One day, at the time when he was destined to be bitten by a snake, he was praying when suddenly something made him stand up. As he did so, his foot hit something sharp and he was cut. There was a sculpture of a serpent in the room. His foot had hit the sharp metal tongue of the snake. The injury happened at the exact time that the snakebite was predicted to occur; but it turned out not to be a real snake, and so there was no poison. The effort he made to deal with the situation, while at the same time surrendering to God, bore fruit. But the other man's life was ruined by his terror before any snakebite had even occurred. So, we should make an effort and do the best that we can, as an offering to God, without blaming fate. Then we will be able to survive any obstacles.

Question – Couldn't Lord Krishna have changed Duryodhana's mind and avoided the war?

Mother – The Lord showed His divine form to both the Pandavas and the Kauravas. Arjuna was able to perceive His greatness, but Duryodhana was not. He committed a sin when he dismissed the vision as Krishna's magic. Whatever a mahatma does, it won't benefit those who refuse to surrender. Spiritual instructions can be given only according to the seeker's qualifications and character. Only the realization of the body (whatever his body-consciousness could give) was important to Duryodhana. He was not ready to hear any spiritual truths. He didn't believe Lord Krishna spoke for his own good; he thought the Lord always favored the Pandavas. War was the only way to destroy the ego of such an adharmic individual as Duryodhana.

Question – Isn't it useless to pray before one's mind has become pure?

Mother – My children, don't think thoughts like, "I have committed so many mistakes in my life. I can't pray because my mind isn't pure enough. I'll start praying as soon as my mind becomes pure." If you decide to swim in the sea only after all the waves have subsided, you will never get to swim. Nor will you learn how to swim by just sitting on the shore. You have to get into the water.

Imagine if a doctor were to say to a patient, "You can come to me only after your illness is gone!" What good would that do? We go to the doctor to get cured of the illness!

God purifies our minds. That is why we take refuge in Him. Only through God can the mind be made pure.

There is no need to feel remorseful about the way we have lived until this moment. The past is like a cancelled check.

A pencil usually comes with an eraser, so that we can quickly erase what we have just written. But we can erase there only once, for if we write again in that spot and then erase again what we have written, we will end up tearing the paper. God forgives us for the mistakes we make out of ignorance, but to repeat a mistake after we have understood it is an error is the gravest type of mistake. We should avoid this.

Question – One notices anger in a lot of people who do spiritual practice. How can that be removed?

Mother – Anger cannot be transcended through meditation or the chanting of a mantra only. Those who spend all their time living in solitude, doing only spiritual practice are like a tree in the scorching heat of a remote desert. The world doesn't benefit from its shade. Such people ought to go out and, living in the midst of the world, try to develop the attitude of seeing God in everyone and everything. If you put rocks of different shapes in a container and tumble them around, the rocks will rub against each other and lose their sharp edges. They will become nice and smooth. Similarly, a seeker should go out into the world, "battle," and develop a mature mind. Only those who succeed in the midst of a world full of diversity can claim to have succeeded.

Courageous are those who refrain from getting angry in situations where anger would be expected. When a person doing spiritual practice in solitude says, "I don't get angry," it doesn't mean anything, nor is it a sign of courage. Your negative tendencies won't necessarily die just because you are doing spiritual practice somewhere alone. A frozen cobra won't raise its hood and bite; but as soon as it is warmed by the sun, its nature changes. The jackal sits in the forest and makes a vow, "From now on, I won't howl when I see a dog!" But as he comes out of the forest and catches the first glimpse of a dog's tail, his vow evaporates. We should be able to maintain our mental control even in the most adverse circumstances. That is where the success of your spiritual practice can be measured. At a certain stage of an aspirant's spiritual practice, the aspirant is like a child confined to a room, and his or her anger often gets a little stronger. This can be overcome by practice in the presence of a master.

Question – Isn't it true that some of the sages used to get angry?

Mother – Their anger destroyed people's egos. Their anger was an expression of their compassion. The anger of a sage cannot be compared to the anger of an ordinary person. The purpose of the master's anger is to remove the tamas (inertia) from the disciple. If a cow eats your precious plants and you approach the animal, gently pleading, "Dear cow, please don't eat that plant. Please go away," the cow won't budge. But if you shout at it sternly, it will move. Your sternness turns the cow, which lacks discrimination, away from the wrong it is doing. Similarly, the anger of a perfect master is just for show; it doesn't come from within. The master's anger is like a soap that cleans the disciple's mind. The master's sole aim is the upward progress of the disciple. A burned rope or a burned lime peel appears to have a form; but it crumbles the moment you touch it. The anger of a sage isn't real; it is a deliberate act meant to turn others to the right path.

Nighttime with Mother at the Backwaters

The reverberating sound of a conch shell signaled the end of the Devi Bhava darshan. It was two o'clock in the morning. The ashram residents had been busy throughout the previous day carrying sand. They were reclaiming some land by filling in the backwaters. Mother had also taken part in the work, and this made everyone very enthusiastic. Today She had given darshan in the big hut and then, after barely two hours, had come out again at five p.m. to sing devotional songs and give Devi Bhava darshan. Only now, after many hours, did She finally stand up again, having given darshan to everyone.

But instead of going to Her room, Mother walked straight to the edge of the backwaters. Not all of the sand that had been brought in had as yet been used. In the morning another barge would arrive carrying more sand. The residents and devotees came running to carry sand along with Mother.

For those who know Mother even a little, such hard toil done while foregoing food and sleep is nothing new. But Mark, who had just come from Germany for the first time to see Mother, couldn't bear this sight. He tried many times to snatch the sack of sand from Mother's arms. But was She ever going to yield?

Creating a little break during the work, She called Mark close to Her. As soon as his eyes fell on Her glorious face, they filled with tears.

"Son, Mother hasn't had the chance to say a word to you until now. Are you unhappy about that?" She asked.

"I am not sad because you haven't spoken to me. I'm sad because I'm seeing you and your children work so hard. Mother, if you will give your blessing, I will give you all of my wealth. I want only that you should rest instead of working day and night like this!"

Mother laughed at Mark's reply.

Mother – Son, this is an ashram, not a holiday resort. This is a place for those who practice self-sacrifice. The ashram residents have to strive hard for the sake of their ideal. This is heaven for those who are spiritually inclined. These children here have led a life of hard work for so long, but none of it seems like hardship to them! Mother told them from the beginning when they first came here that they would have to be like candles. A candle allows itself to melt down so that it can give light to others. Similarly, our self-sacrifice is the light of the world; it is the light of the Self.

Think of how many people are suffering in this world. Think of all the sick, impoverished people living in pain, with no money for treatment or medicines; the countless who are destitute, desperately struggling to survive, unable to get even a single meal. And there are so many children who have to break off their studies because their families can't pay for their education. We can use what we save from our wages to help people in need. In our orphanage there are about five hundred children. We have to be willing to help others, even if it means that we ourselves have to undergo some hardships.

Everybody likes a job where you sit in an office chair and work. No one wants to do this type of work. Shouldn't we be role models for others? Didn't the Lord say in the Bhagavad Gita, "Equanimity is yoga"? We should view any type work as a way of worshipping God. If these children see Mother doing this work today, they won't hesitate to do any type of work tomorrow. The Self is eternal. To know the Self you have to totally eradicate body-consciousness. But this is possible only through renunciation. Those who live selflessly can transform any situation into a favorable one.

Son, who can do spiritual practice all twenty four hours of the day? The time that is left after spiritual practice should be used to do good deeds. That will help to reduce your thoughts. This world that you see is truly the satguru's body. To love the master is to work according to the master's directions. Selfless work is also a form of spiritual practice. Those who lead completely selfless lives don't need any additional spiritual practice. Son, only through renunciation can you attain immortality.

Question – Hasn't God given us this body and created the objects of the world so that we can enjoy them and live in happiness?

Mother – If you drive your car just any way you feel like, disregarding the rules of the road, you will probably have an accident and could even die. There are rules of the road which have to be followed. Similarly, not only has God created everything; He has laid down rules for everything, and we have to live according to those rules or we will come to regret it.

Eat only what is necessary. Speak only when necessary. Sleep only for as long as you need. Spend the remaining time doing good deeds. Do not waste a single moment in life. Try to make your life beneficial for others as well.

If you eat as much chocolate as you please, you will get a stomach ache. Too much of anything will cause problems. We need to understand that worldly happiness causes suffering.

Question – Isn't God making us do everything?

Mother – God has given us intelligence—the intelligence to use our discrimination. We should use that intelligence and perform our actions with discrimination. God has also created poison, but no one would take poison for no reason. With something like that, we don't hesitate to use our discrimination. We need to weigh our every action in the same manner.

Question – Mother, aren't those who surrender to a spiritual master weak-minded?

Mother – When you press down a button, the umbrella unfolds. Similarly, by bowing your head down before a spiritual master, your mind can be transformed into the universal Mind. Such obedience and humbleness are not a sign of weakness. Like a purifying water filter, the master purifies your mind and removes your ego. People helplessly become slaves of their egos in every situation. They don't proceed with discrimination.

One night a thief broke into a house, but as he entered the building the people woke up and he fled. The local residents ran after him shouting, "Thief! There goes the thief! Catch him!" As a crowd gathered, the thief joined in. He ran with the crowd shouting at the top of his voice, "Thief! Thief!" Similarly, our ego joins our company at every turn. Even when God gives us opportunities to discard the ego, we nurture it instead and make it our companion. People seldom attempt to get rid of the ego by being humble.

Today, people's minds are weak, like a plant growing in a pot. If the plant isn't watered daily, the plant withers the very next day. The mind cannot be brought under your control without discipline and certain rules. As long as you haven't mastered your mind, you need to abide by certain rules and restraints according to the master's instructions. Once you have mastered your mind, there is nothing to fear; for then the power of discrimination will awaken within you and lead you forward.

A man once went in search of a master. He wanted a guru who could guide him according to his own desires. But no guru was willing to do that; nor were the rules they imposed acceptable to him. In the end, he was tired and lay down in a field to rest. He thought, "There's no guru who can guide me the way I like. I refuse to become anyone's slave! Whatever I choose to do, isn't it God who is making me do it anyway?" He turned his head to the side and saw a camel standing nearby, nodding its head. "Ah, yes! There is someone who is fit to be my master!" he thought.

"O camel, will you be my master?" he asked. The camel nodded its head.

So he accepted the camel as his spiritual master. "O master, may I take you home?" he asked. The camel nodded again. He took it home and tied it to a tree. A few days passed. "O master, there's a girl I'm in love with. May I marry her?" he asked. The camel nodded. "O master, I have no children," he said. The camel nodded again. Children were born.

"May I drink a little alcohol with my friends?" the man asked. The camel nodded. The fellow soon became a drunkard. He started quarrelling with his wife.

"O master, my wife is bothering me. May I kill her?" he asked the camel. The camel nodded. He killed his wife. The police came and arrested him. He was imprisoned for life.

Son, if you find a guru who lets you do whatever you want, or if you just live as you please, you will end up in bondage. We all have a discriminating intelligence given to us by God. We should use it in our actions. We should follow the master's words. A true master lives only for the sake of his or her disciples.

Only non-duality is real. But that isn't something to be explained in words. It is life itself. It is an experience. It is something that has to come from within. When the flower blossoms, a fragrance will emanate from the flower of its own accord.

Question – I don't understand what is wrong with enjoying the objects of the senses that God has created. Hasn't God given us the senses in the first place so that we can enjoy those things?

Mother – As Mother said, there are rules and limits

for everything, and we should live in harmony with those rules. Everything has its own inherent nature. God has given humans not only their senses but also a discriminating intelligence. Those who don't use their power of discrimination but instead run after the senses in search of pleasure will never find peace or happiness. They will always end up suffering.

A traveler once arrived in a foreign country. It was his first visit to that land. The people there were total strangers. He didn't know the language, nor was he familiar with the local customs or eating habits. He walked along the streets taking in the sights around him until he came to a market place with a big crowd of shoppers. There were many different fruits of various sizes and colors on display, most of which he had never seen before. He noticed that a lot of people were buying one particular fruit. He imagined it must be very sweet and juicy if it was that popular, and so he bought a bagful. He went and sat down under a tree, took one of the fruits out of the bag and bit into it. But it wasn't sweet at all! It burned his mouth like fire! He tasted the middle portion. That, too, was hot. Thinking that the other side of the fruit must surely be sweet, he bit into that end as well. But that was just as hot. He tried another fruit. It burned like fire. He thought that at least one of the fruits in the packet must be sweet, and tried another one. That too was hot and not sweet at all. But he refused to give up. Tears were streaming from his eyes, but he stubbornly kept eating the fruits, expecting to find at least one that was sweet and juicy, until he had finally finished them all. The poor man was in agony! He longed for sweetness, but all he got was burning-hot fire. What he assumed to be sweet fruits were ripe hot chili peppers! It would have been all right had he discarded them after tasting one or two and discovering how hot they were. There was no need for him to suffer like that. But in the hope of finding the sweetness he longed for in one of them, he kept eating till the very last one was gone. And so he suffered. Fiery hotness is the very nature of a chili pepper. The only pleasure those fruits gave him was the external pleasure of looking at them.

People look for happiness in things whose essential nature is not happiness at all. They go from one object to another. It is just an illusion of the mind to think that you can get happiness from any external object. In truth, there is no happiness to be found in anything outside. The happiness you long for exists within you. God has given us a body, senses, and intelligence, so that we can learn this lesson and search for the real source of bliss. If we use our senses indiscriminately, we will experience only suffering instead of the happiness we expect.

The body and the senses can be used in two different ways. If we strive to know God, we can enjoy eternal bliss; but if we run only after sensory pleasures, our experience will be the same as that of the traveler who searched for sweetness in the burning-hot chilies.

If we run after sense pleasures without understanding that their inherent nature is suffering, we will have to suffer the misery that arises from them. If we understand the essential nature of external objects, we won't be debilitated by suffering.

The ocean waves rise up and then crash onto the beach a moment later. They cannot stay up. Similarly, the person who eagerly pursues external objects, hoping to find happiness that way, falls into a state of suffering. The mind leaps up in search of happiness, but doesn't find true happiness—only suffering. From this we can learn that happiness is not to be found externally.

The quest for happiness in the material world is the cause of people's suffering and lack of inner peace. This affects not only the individual but society as a whole. Because of humanity's quest for happiness in external things, real love has disappeared. Joy and peace have vanished from family life. People have lost their ability to love and to serve others with open hearts. Husbands desire other women, and wives desire other men. It has gone so far that in their excessive desire for pleasure, there are men who forget that their own daughters are their daughters. Even the concept of the brother-sister relationship is crumbling. Countless children are being murdered. The reason for all this evil we see in the world today is the total misconception that happiness can be found externally.

Mother is not saying that you should deny yourselves any pleasures. But you should recognize their real nature. Nothing should be done in excess. Dharma should never be forsaken. Adharma should be shunned.

For those who crave only selfish pleasures and live without any restraints, the result will be ruin. It is natural that desires and emotions arise in the mind, but some restraint is necessary. It is natural to feel hungry, but we don't eat whenever we catch sight of something edible. If we did, we would get sick. Likewise, the craving for excessive pleasures leads to suffering. People don't realize this. The pleasure they get from the senses actually comes from within themselves. People chase frantically after external happiness until they collapse in a state of suffering and despair. Then, again they run around and again they collapse. If you go in search of external pleasures only, you won't find peace in life. You have to learn to look inward, for that is where real bliss is to be found. But you won't find that bliss until your mind's outward leaps are stopped and the mind becomes still. In the depth of the ocean there are no waves. Similarly, you will find that the mind automatically becomes still as you enter into the depths of your mind. Then there is only bliss.

Question – Spiritual masters seem to give greater importance to the heart than to the intellect. But isn't the intellect actually more important? How can one possibly achieve any goal without the intellect?

Mother – The intellect is necessary. Mother never says that you don't need it. But, the intellect often doesn't function in a person when the occasion calls for doing a good deed. It is selfishness that comes to the forefront and not the discriminating intellect.

The heart and the intellect are not two separate things. When you have a discriminating intellect, you will naturally become expansive. From that expansiveness, a spirit of innocence, compromise, humbleness, and a willingness to help others will naturally arise. The word "heart" stands for that expansiveness. Even at the very mention of the word "heart," we feel a soothing gentleness. However, in most people today we see only an ordinary intellect, not a discriminating one. What we see is not really intellect, but ego. The ego is the cause of all the suffering in life. As the ego grows, the person's expansiveness contracts and the spirit of compromise disappears. One cannot do without these qualities, either in spiritual life or in worldly life.

Let Mother ask you something, son. Suppose you set up rules in your family: "My wife should live like this, should talk like this, and behave in this way, because she belongs to me." Will there be peace at home if you insist that she lives according to those rules? No. Suppose you come home from the office. You don't say a word to your wife or children; you go straight to your room and continue your work, still acting like the official you are at the office. Will your family be pleased? If you declare that this is simply the way you are, will they be able to accept that? Will there be peace?

If instead you exchange warm greetings with your wife as you enter the house and spend some time with your children—if you are ready to give a little of yourself and not be so one-sided—everyone will be pleased. When we tolerate and forgive one another's faults and shortcomings, there will be peace and happiness in the family. When you treat your marriage partner's shortcomings very lightly, it is because of your love for that person. Even if your loved one makes mistakes, you still love her. Aren't you giving more importance to the heart in that case? Isn't it because the two of you feel that your hearts are as one that you are able to spend your lives together? It is this attitude that Mother calls "heart."

Would it be practical to insist on following a list of rules in our behavior toward our children? Will the children yield to our likes and dislikes? Won't they react by being stubborn?

Because of our love for our children, we tolerate their mistakes, and bring them up properly. So the heart is more important than the intellect here, too, isn't it? When this is so, we experience happiness during every moment we spend with our children, and we make them happy.

Only when people's hearts are open toward one another do they find happiness in family life. If the intellect is allowed to eclipse the role of the heart, we won't experience any happiness. We can use the intellect in the market place or at work because there it is required of us. But that won't work when you are with your family. Even in the office some amount of openheartedness and compromise is necessary. If we ignore this, there will be only discord and unhappiness.

When we allow the heart a place in our lives, an attitude of compromise, the flexibility of "give and take," is born in us. With the power of discrimination, expansiveness and a spirit of compromise will naturally arise. Today people's intellects stay solely within the confines of their self-centeredness; their power of discrimination has not been developed. This is a great deficiency in people's lives. It is difficult for society to progress without compromise. The spirit of compromise leads to peace.

Just as we have to apply grease to a rusty machine to make it function properly, for there to be unhindered progress in our lives, humility and the spirit of compromise are essential. But these qualities will be born within us only if we develop our hearts. There are situations where the intellect is needed, but only there should it be brought to bear. In any situation where the heart should be given a prominent place, we shouldn't fail to accord it that place.

When you construct a house, the deeper the foundation you lay, the taller the building can be. Similarly, our humbleness and large-heartedness are the foundation of our upward progress. When we give the heart a prominent place in our lives, humbleness and a spirit of compromise develops within us. Our relationships will be positive and peaceful.

The goal of spirituality also includes an expansion of heart, because only those who are large-hearted can know God. The essence of the Self lies beyond logic and intellect. No matter how much sugar you eat, you can't explain exactly how sweet it is to those who have never tasted sugar. Nor can words describe the infinite sky. You cannot measure the fragrance of a flower. Spirituality is beyond words—it is an experience. You cannot savor its sweetness without going beyond the intellect to the heart.

There is a story about a poor farmer who stood outside his hut one day when a crowd passed by. When he asked where they were heading, they said, "A three-day discourse on the Bhagavad Gita is about to begin nearby. We are all going there." The farmer wanted to hear the discourse, too. So he joined the crowd. When he got there, the place was filled with people. Most of the participants were wealthy and wore expensive clothes and jewelry. The farmer was dirty from his work and was wearing his soiled, tattered old clothes. The people at the door refused to let him in. The farmer was very distressed. He prayed, "Lord, I came to hear your story. But these people won't let me in. Am I so worthless that I don't even deserve to hear your story? Am I such a sinner? Well, then, if this is Your will, let it be so. I'll just sit here outside and listen to Your tale."

And so, he went and sat under a mango tree and listened to the discourse from there. But he couldn't understand anything because it was all in Sanskrit. The poor man felt heartbroken. He called out, "O Lord, I can't even understand Your language! Am I such a great sinner?" At that moment, his eyes fell on a large picture displayed in front of the hall. The picture depicted Lord Krishna holding the reins in one hand as He expounded the Bhagavad Gita to Arjuna, who was sitting behind him in the chariot. The farmer sat there, gazing at the Lord's face. His eyes filled with tears. He didn't know for how long he sat there. When he finally looked up, the discourse had ended and the participants were leaving. The farmer went home. The next day he returned to the venue. He couldn't stop thinking about the Lord's face. His only aim was to sit there under the tree and look at that picture. On the third day of the discourse, he again came and sat beneath the tree and gazed entranced at the picture. His eyes overflowed with tears. He experienced the Lord's form shining brightly within him. He closed his eyes and sat there beholding Lord Krishna, forgetting himself.

The crowd dispersed after the discourse that day. When the scholar who had given the lecture came out, he saw the farmer sitting motionless under the mango tree. Tears were coursing down the farmer's cheeks. The scholar was astonished. He thought, "Why is this man sitting here and weeping even after the discourse has ended? Did my talk move him so?" He approached the farmer. The farmer sat very still. From the expression on his face, it was clear that he was brimming with bliss. There was a sense of perfect peace around him. The scholar aroused the farmer and asked, "Did you enjoy my discourse that much?"

The farmer replied, "I haven't understood a word of what you've said during these past three days, sir! I don't know Sanskrit. But when I think of the Lord's condition, I feel overwhelmed with grief. Didn't the Lord say all those things while looking backward? His shoulder must have hurt so much as He kept His head turned back like that! That's why I am crying like this." It is said that the farmer attained enlightenment as he uttered those words.

It was the farmer's compassion and innocence that made him eligible for Self-realization. As he listened to the farmer's words, the scholar's own eyes filled with tears and he experienced a peace he had never known until that moment.

The man who gave the discourse was a highly intelligent man. The people in the audience were also well-educated. But it was the poor, innocent farmer who was able to savor the sweetness of devotion and became qualified for realization. His was an example of selfless compassion. His grief was not about himself, but about the perceived hardship of the Lord.

When people visit a temple, they often pray, "Please give me this and that." But the farmer experienced a compassion that was beyond all that. There was no ego in him. Normally, it is difficult to get rid of the sense of "I", but because of his innocence, he lost his individuality. He experienced parabhakti (supreme devotion). That is the highest state. He was qualified for that because, in contrast to the others who were functioning from their intellects, he was functioning from his heart. As a result, he became immersed in bliss, effortlessly and spontaneously, and was able to radiate some of that peace to those around him. It is through our hearts that we should try to know God, for it is there that He shines. God lives in our hearts.

The flow of Mother's words slowed and merged in a sea of silence. Her eyes, which by now were filled with tears of bliss, closed slowly. The tears moistened that face of compassion. There was a small group of devotees sitting around Her; no one uttered a word. Mark was silent and closed his eyes in meditation. All the others stopped what they were doing and came and sat down close to Mother. In that atmosphere of pure bliss their thoughts subsided and dissolved. Minds dissolved into an indescribably sublime experience.

Later, the conversation continued.

Question – If a person's desire to serve the spiritual master is greater than the desire for realization, will the master be with that person during all his or her future lives?

Mother – If that is the desire of a disciple who has surrendered completely to the master, then the master will definitely be with him or her. But the disciple mustn't waste even a second. He or she has to be like an incense stick that burns itself down in order to spread fragrance to others. The disciple's every breath should be for the sake of the world. With every action such a disciple should have the attitude that he or she is serving the master. One who has taken complete refuge in a spiritual master has no more lives to live, unless he or she is born again because it is the master's will.

But there are many types of teachers. There are those who give instructions after studying the scriptures and the

Puranas. They are gurus. Today people who have read just any book and profess anything whatsoever are also considered to be gurus. But a satguru, a real guru, is quite different. A true master is someone who has realized the truth through austerities and renunciation, and has directly experienced the supreme state described in the scriptures. Outwardly, he or she may not look special when compared to others, but the benefits you get from such a master cannot be had from those who merely pretend to be gurus. Those who show much outward pomp and splendor may not have much at their core; you won't benefit much by depending on them. The difference between them and a satguru is like the difference between a ten-watt bulb and a thousand-watt bulb. The very presence of a real master will fill you with bliss and weaken your vasanas.

The teachings of the satgurus are not confined to their words. Their words are reflected in their actions. In their lives you can see the living words of the scriptures. If you study their lives, there is no real need to study the scriptures. The satgurus are utterly selfless. They can be compared to an image made of chocolate or rock candy, because from them comes only pure sweetness—nothing is to be discarded. The satgurus have taken birth solely for the purpose of uplifting the world. They are not individuals; they represent an ideal. We need only follow in their path. The great masters open our eyes of wisdom and remove the darkness.

God is present in everything. But it is the satguru who corrects our mistakes and raises us to God's world. That is why the master is said to be Brahma, Vishnu, and Maheshwara.[21] The satguru means even more to the disciple than God. Once you find a satguru, you no longer need to think about realization, nor do you need to worry about rebirth. All you need to do is follow the path of your master. Just like a pond that has joined a river merging into the sea, once you have come to the master, you have reached the place where you need to be. The master will look after the rest and will take you to the goal. All the disciple needs to do is surrender wholeheartedly at the master's feet. The master will never forsake the disciple.

Question – Mother, what path is most suitable in this age for attaining self-realization?

Mother – Self-realization is not something that is sitting out there somewhere. According to Lord Krishna, equanimity is yoga. We should be able to see everything as Divine Consciousness. Only then can we attain perfection. We should also see only good in everything. A honey bee focuses only on the nectar in a flower and enjoys its sweetness. Only those who always see the good side in everything are eligible for realization.

If we really desire realization, we should be able to forget the body completely. We have to be absolutely convinced that we are the Self. God doesn't have any special dwelling place; God dwells in our hearts. We have to rid ourselves of all attachments and body-consciousness. That is all that is needed. And with this, a profound understanding will take root in us: that the Self has no birth or death, no happiness or sorrow. All fear of death will dissolve and we will be filled with bliss.

21 In Hinduism the Godhead is a trinity—Brahma (the Creator), Vishnu (the Preserver), and Shiva or Maheshwara (the Destroyer).

A seeker should learn to welcome every situation with patience. If honey is mixed with salt, the saltiness can be removed by continuously adding honey. In the same way, we have to remove every trace of animosity and the sense of "I" from within us. We do this by thinking good thoughts. When the mind thus becomes pure, we will be able to welcome any situation with joy. In this way we will make spiritual progress, though we may not even be aware of our progress.

In the state of Self-realization we see others as our own Self. If we slip on something and fall, hurting our foot, we don't blame our eyes for being careless and destroy them! We try to comfort our foot. If our left hand is injured, our right hand reaches out to comfort it. Similarly, to forgive those who make mistakes, because we experience our own Self in them—that is Self-realization.

For the realized one, nothing is separate from the Self. But without having reached that state, all talk of Self-realization is just words, and those words won't be imbued with the power of experience. But it is impossible to attain this level of consciousness, this level of experience, without the help of a satguru. All that needs to be done is to follow the master's words.

Self-realization isn't something you can buy somewhere. Your attitude has to be transformed, that's all. People mistakenly believe the bondage they are in is real. There is a story about a cow that was normally kept tethered in the cowshed. One day, she wasn't tied up; she was just led into the cowshed and the door was closed. The rope was left lying on the floor. The next day when the owner opened the door to the cowshed to let the cow out, the cow didn't move. He pushed her, but she refused to budge. He beat her with a stick but even then she stood still. Then he thought, "I usually untie the rope when I come in, but I didn't tie her up last night. What if I act as if I were untying her?" He picked up the end of the rope and pretended to untie the cow from the usual post. The cow immediately left the cowshed. People are in much the same situation as that cow. They are not bound, yet they think they are. You have to remove that illusion. You just have to understand that you are really not in bondage at all. But you won't be able to change that misconception without the help of a real master. This doesn't mean that the master brings you Self-realization. The master's task is to convince you that you are not in bondage. Only if you were actually bound would the bonds have to be untied.

Only when the waves subside can we see the image of the sun on the water. Similarly, only when the waves of the mind subside, can we see the Self. There is no need to create an image; all we need to do is make the waves subside and the image will be revealed.

You cannot see a reflection on clear, transparent glass. One side of the glass has to be covered with a certain paint. Similarly, only when the paint of selflessness is applied within us can we see God.

As long as the ego remains, we cannot become selfless. The master leads the disciple through situations that are necessary to remove the ego. The disciple learns to chisel away the ego. Because of the disciple's proximity to the master and the counsel he receives from the master, the disciple develops patience without even being aware of it. The master puts the disciple in situations in which his patience is tested and his anger may arise. The disciple is given the type of work he doesn't like. This will make the disciple angry and he will disobey. Then the master will encourage the disciple to reflect. The disciple will find within himself the strength needed to transcend difficult situations. Thus the master uses different situations to eliminate the weaknesses of the disciple and to make him strong. This enables the disciple to transcend the ego. It is for the purpose of eliminating the ego that we take refuge in a master.

Only when a conch shell is emptied of the flesh that was inside it can any sound come out of it when it is blown. Similarly, when we become free of the ego, we can rise to our spiritual goal. Once complete surrender has taken place, there is no longer any sense of "I"—there is only God. That state cannot be described in words.

If, after coming to a master, you are preoccupied with thoughts about when you are going to attain realization, it means that you haven't totally surrendered to the master. It means that your faith in the master is not complete. Once you have come to the master, you should follow his or her instructions to the letter, forgetting all other thoughts. That is all the disciple has to do. A true disciple surrenders to the master even the desire for Self-realization. His or her only goal is complete obedience to the master. The master is perfection itself. There are no words to describe the love and reverence the disciple feels toward the master.

Question – If we suffer a downfall even after living with a master, will the master be there to save us in our next life?

Mother – Always follow the master's words. Dedicate yourself totally at his or her feet, and thenceforth see everything as the master's will. As a disciple you shouldn't even think about the possibility of suffering a downfall. Thinking that way reveals a weakness; it means that you have no real faith in yourself. And if you don't believe in yourself, how can you have faith in the master? The master will not forsake the disciple who prays to the master sincerely. The disciple should take total refuge in the master.

Question – What is meant by real service to the master?

Mother – When we talk about a true master, we don't mean just an individual; we mean the Divine Consciousness—the Truth. The master permeates the entire universe. We need to understand this, for only then can we advance spiritually. A disciple should never be attached to the physical body of the master. We should broaden our view so that we see every sentient and insentient being as the master, and serve others with devotion. It is through our bond with the master that we acquire this expansiveness. The mind of a disciple who matures by listening to the master's words and watching the master's deeds rises to that plane without the disciple being aware of it. On the other hand, the service rendered by a person who desires physical proximity to the master for purely selfish reasons is not real service to the master.

The disciple's bond with the master should be such that it becomes impossible to be away from the master even for a moment. At the same time, you should be expansive enough to serve others, and should do this to the point of forgetting yourself. You should serve others with the attitude that you are serving the master. Such is the true disciple who has absorbed the real essence of the master. The master will always be with such a disciple.

When we see a mango tree, our attention is not on the tree but on the fruits. Yet we don't neglect to take care of the tree. Similarly, although a disciple knows well that the master is not the body but is truly the all-pervasive Consciousness, still the master's body is precious, and personal service to the master is dearer to a disciple than life itself. As a true disciple, you find that you are ready to give up your life for the master's sake. And yet, your concept of the master is not confined to the limited individual. You see your master in all living beings. And thus, you actually see that to serve anyone is to serve the master. The true disciple gets contentment and happiness from this.

Question – If the master isn't realized, what is the benefit of surrendering to him? Will the disciple not be cheated? How can we determine whether a spiritual teacher is realized or not?

Mother – That is hard to say. Everyone wants to become whoever is the biggest movie star at the moment. People will do anything to achieve this. They try all forms of imitation. Similarly, there are many people who want to pose as masters when they see the honor and respect accorded a spiritual master. If we were to list the signs of a perfect master, it would make it easier for those who are eager to take on the role of a master; ordinary people would be swindled by their charades. So it is best not to elaborate on the nature of a satguru. It shouldn't be discussed publicly.

The scriptures have given certain descriptions of the characteristics of a master. However, it is difficult to use the characteristics seen in one master as a criterion when trying to discern whether or not another person is a true master. Each master acts in his or her own way. However much you read and study, it is difficult to find a perfect master unless you have a pure heart. Renunciation, love, compassion, and selflessness can generally be found in all masters. But a master takes on very different roles to test the disciples. Only a pure-hearted disciple can take this. When the seeker starts searching with genuine longing and a pure heart, a real master will come to him or her. But the master will also test the disciple.

Even if a seeker falls into the hands of a false master, if the seeker's heart is pure, his innocence will nevertheless lead him to the goal. God will clear the path required for this.

Instead of wasting time testing and comparing masters, it is better to pray to God to help you to become a perfect disciple and lead you to a perfect master. Only when the intellect and the heart merge can a disciple really recognize a true master.

Question – Mother, in what ways does the master test his or her disciples?

Mother – We cannot list a general set of rules for that, like the guidelines for success in an examination. The master leads the disciple according to the vasanas the disciple has acquired during many lifetimes. Even in identical situations, the master may behave quite differently toward different disciples. It won't necessarily make any sense to you. Only the master will know the reason. The master decides which procedures to follow to weaken the vasanas of a particular individual and to lead him or her to the goal. The one factor that will help the disciple's spiritual progress is that he or she yield to the master's decision.

When two disciples make the same mistake, the master may get angry with one of them and be very loving toward the other, acting as though nothing has happened. The master knows the level of mental strength and maturity in each disciple. Because of their ignorance, onlookers may criticize the master. They see only what is happening outwardly. They lack the insight to see the changes taking place in the disciples.

The tree can't emerge until the outer shell of the seed breaks. Similarly, you cannot know the Truth without totally destroying the ego. The master will test the disciple in various ways to ascertain whether he or she has come to the master out of a short-lived surge of enthusiasm or out of love for the spiritual goal. Those tests can be compared to surprise tests in the classroom; there is no advance warning. It is the master's duty to measure how much patience, renunciation, and compassion the disciple has, and to test whether he or she becomes weak when faced with certain situations, or has the strength to overcome them. The disciples are expected to provide the world with leadership in the future. Thousands of people may come to them one day, placing their complete trust in them. The disciples have to possess enough inner strength, maturity, and compassion to live up to that trust. If a disciple goes out into the world without those qualities, and lacks enough inner purity, that will be the greatest type of betrayal. As a result, the one who is supposed to protect the world could become a destructive enemy instead.

The master makes the disciple go through numerous tests to mold him or her properly.

A master once gave his disciple a rock and asked him to sculpt an image. The obedient disciple gave up food and sleep and set to work carving an image. When it was completed he brought the image to the master and offered it at his feet. He stood aside humbly with joined palms and bowed head. The master glanced at the sculpture, picked it up, and flung it away. It broke into several pieces. "Is this the way to make an image?" he asked angrily. The disciple looked at the broken pieces and thought, "He didn't utter one kind word, even though I have worked so hard for days without food or sleep!" Knowing his thoughts, the master gave him another stone and asked him to start again and sculpt another image. The disciple went away with the stone and made a new image more beautiful than the first one. Again, he approached the master, thinking that this time the master would surely be pleased. But as soon as the master saw the image, his face reddened. "Are you making fun of me?" he said. "This one is worse than the last one!" And he broke that image as well. He looked at the disciple who was standing there with his head bowed humbly. This time the disciple didn't feel any resentment toward the master, but he did feel a little sad. The master gave him another stone and asked him to make a new piece. The disciple sculpted the new image with much care. It was a great work of art. He submitted it at the master's feet. But the master picked it up and shattered it in an instant, severely scolding the disciple. This time the disciple felt neither angry nor sad. He thought, "If this is my master's wish, let it be so. Everything he does is for my own good." Such was his attitude of surrender at that point. The master gave him yet another stone. The disciple accepted it with joy and came back with another exceptionally beautiful image. The master broke that one as well. But there was not the slightest change in the disciple's mood. The master was very pleased. He placed his hands on the disciple's head and blessed him. An observer looking at the master's actions would probably think the master was being cruel or even crazy. Only the master and the disciple who had completely surrendered to him could know what was really taking place. Each time the master smashed an image the disciple brought to him, he was sculpting a real image in the heart of the disciple. It was the disciple's ego that was being broken. Only a satguru can do this, and only a true disciple can taste the bliss that comes from it.

The disciple needs to understand that the master knows far better than the disciple what is good or bad for the disciple, and what the disciple does or does not need. One should never approach a master seeking position or fame. You go to a master because you wish to surrender yourself. If you feel any anger or resentment when the master doesn't praise you or your actions, then you lack the qualifications needed to be a disciple. Pray that your anger be removed. Understand that the master's every action is for your own good.

Some people think, "For how many years have I been

with my master? And yet my master keeps treating me this way!" This just shows their lack of surrender. Only those who surrender not just a few years, but all of their lifetimes at the master's feet are true disciples. When the attitude "I am the body, mind, and intellect" persists, anger, aversion, and egoism arise in the mind. It is to get rid of those negative qualities that a seeker takes refuge in a spiritual master. Unless we surrender completely to the master, there is no way we can overcome our negativities. The attitude that everything the master does is for our own good has to take firm hold in the mind. We should never allow the intellect to judge any of the master's actions.

My children, no one can predict what form the master's tests will take. To totally surrender is the only way to pass those tests. They are verily proof of the master's compassion toward the disciple. They weaken the disciple's vasanas. Only through self-surrender can you gain the master's grace.

A youth approached a master, requesting to be accepted as a disciple. The master said, "Son, you don't have the mental maturity required to lead a completely spiritual life. You have some prarabdha that still has to be exhausted. Wait a little longer."

But the young man refused to back down. Because of his insistence, the master finally accepted him as a disciple. Some time later the master gave sannyasa initiation to all of his disciples except this one. The disciple couldn't bear this. He was angry with the master. He didn't show it outwardly, but he started talking negatively about the master to the visitors who came to the ashram. The master knew this, but didn't say anything. After a while, the disciple started voicing his criticism even in the master's presence. The master knew the disciple's nature very well. He knew that no amount of advice would change him, that he would learn only from experience. So he kept quiet.

Around that time, the master decided to conduct a great yajna (sacrifice) for the welfare of the world. Many items were needed as offerings to the sacred fire during the sacrifice. A family near the ashram volunteered to provide everything needed. The young man was given the job of fetching the items every day during the course of the yajna. A young woman in the family handed him the materials each day. The first time he saw her, the disciple felt attracted to the young woman. His feelings grew stronger as the days passed. One day he couldn't control his mind and he took hold of her hand. The woman didn't hesitate for an instant. She picked up a stick that was lying on the ground and hit him in the face.

As soon as the master saw the disciple coming back with his face covered, he understood what had happened. He said, "Do you see now why I didn't want to accept you as a disciple in the beginning, and why I didn't make you a sannyasi? Think of how shameful it would have been had you acted that way wearing the ochre robe! That would have been a great betrayal of the world and of the lineage of sannyasis. Go and live in the world for some time, son. I will call you when the time comes." Only then did the disciple finally understand his mistake and he prostrated at the master's feet.

You don't become a first-rate doctor just by getting a medical degree. You also have to serve as an intern with an experienced doctor, and gain experience in treating various illnesses. Only through hard work and constant practice can you become a really good doctor. Similarly, however much you study the spiritual texts, there are invaluable lessons to be learned from going out into the world and working constantly with people. That is the most important way of learning. The satguru will arrange all the circumstances needed for the progress of the disciple who seeks spiritual instructions from him or her. Your vasanas won't die away if you just sit with your eyes closed and meditate. Your mental impurities will be eliminated only if you have complete faith in the master, and if you have the humility and broadness of mind needed to surrender. Surrender is like a bleach that removes stains from your clothes. Surrender removes your mental impurities and vasanas. Contrary to what some people think, surrendering to a satguru is not a form of slavery; it is the gateway to true independence and freedom.

Whatever the temptations may be, the disciple's mind should be steady—that is real surrender to the master. That attitude cannot be bought with any amount of money; it has to develop naturally.

When the disciple has developed this type of surrender, he or she is complete in all respects.

Question – Doesn't the spiritual master understand the disciple's nature as soon as he or she sees the disciple? Then what are all those tests for?

Mother – The master knows the disciple's nature better than the disciple does. And the disciple has to be made aware of his or her own deficiencies. Only then will the aspirant be able to transcend them and go forward.

These days, it is hard to find disciples who really obey

their spiritual master and have a true awareness of the goal. This is an age in which the spiritual master is blamed and criticized if he or she doesn't yield to the disciple's selfishness. Still, out of their infinite compassion, the masters will try their utmost to bring the disciples to the right path. In the old days, the disciple waited patiently before the master. Today, it is the master who waits before the disciple. The master's sole aim is to take the disciple to the supreme state by whichever means necessary. The master is ready to make any sacrifice for this.

You may ask, "Isn't it slavery to obey the master's every word?" But that "slavery" doesn't harm the disciple in any way; on the contrary, it will make the disciple free forever! It helps to awaken the Self within the disciple. For a seed to grow into a majestic tree, it first has to go beneath the soil.

If we waste the seeds and eat them, it will satisfy our hunger for a little while. It is far more beneficial if we plant them and allow them to grow into trees. They will give enough fruits to feed people for years. They will provide cooling shade to passersby who are fatigued from the scorching heat of the sun. Even while someone is cutting down a tree, the tree provides that person with shade.

We should surrender to the master instead of yielding to our ego. By doing this, we will be able to alleviate the suffering of countless people later. Surrendering to the master, obeying the master, is never slavery—it is a sign of courage. A truly courageous person surrenders to the spiritual master in order to eradicate the ego.

We cling to a small piece of land, putting a fence around it, calling it our own. Because of this attachment we give up our sovereignty over the entire universe. We need only get rid of the sense of "I." Then, all the three worlds will kneel before us. Today, the greatest difficulty for a master is to find worthy disciples. Many of today's disciples are the type of people who spend a short time with the master, and then they, themselves, want to set up an ashram and pose as masters. If there are two people who prostrate before them, those disciples put on airs. Being aware of this, the master tries to remove the disciple's ego completely. Remember that every situation created by the perfect master is a gift of grace, meant to remove the ego that disfigures the personality of the disciple, and to reveal the beauty of the Self within him or her. This is the path toward ultimate freedom, divinity, and everlasting peace.

Conversations with Mother

Question – Mother, we go to temples and we come to you. Is that enough for our spiritual progress, or do we also have to meditate and repeat a mantra?

Mother – My children, don't think you will get peace of mind just by coming here, even if you do so for years, or by visiting a temple a thousand times. It is meaningless to blame God, complaining that you have been going to a temple for forty years and have not experienced any benefit. As long as your heart has not become pure, there won't be any benefit. It is useless to visit the ashram if you just keep thinking of the things you have to do when you get home, and feel impatient to leave. When you visit a temple or come here, repeat your mantra, do archana (chant the divine names), meditate, or sing devotional songs. Only then will you benefit. Tune your heart to the realm of God. No one attains liberation just by going to Benares or Tiruppati[22] to bathe there and circumambulate. If people automatically attained liberation just by going to Tiruppati, then everyone with businesses there would be liberated, wouldn't they? And wouldn't every murderer and robber

22 Benares is considered one of the holiest places in India. Tirupatti is one of the foremost pilgrim places in South India, where there is a famous temple dedicated to Lord Venkeshwara (Lord Vishnu).

who happened to live in Benares also get liberation? Our hearts should be purified; only then will we benefit from going anywhere. But that rarely happens these days.

Concrete will set properly only if the "metal"[23] used is pure. Similarly, only when our hearts are pure can God be established within us. Only if we focus the mind on God, for example, by chanting a mantra, meditating, or praying, will the mind become purified.

A television station broadcasts various programs, but we have to tune the TV properly to receive those programs. If we don't select the right channel, why blame others for our not being able to see anything? God's grace is always with us. But to receive that grace, we first have to tune ourselves to the realm of God. If we don't bother to do this, there is no point in blaming God. As long as we are not in tune with God's realm, there will only be discordant notes of ignorance within us, not God's divine music. God is definitely compassionate. Let us try to mold our hearts. This is what is needed.

Question – Mother, I have found no peace or happiness in life. There is only sorrow. I can't help wondering why I should continue to live.

Mother – Daughter, your ego is the cause of your grief. God, who is the very source of peace and happiness, exists within us. We can know God only by doing spiritual practice and relinquishing the ego. Say that you complain that you can't take one more step in the sun, because you are too exhausted from the heat. Yet, all the while you have been carrying an umbrella under your arm! That is

23 Broken stones ("road metal") used in concrete for building and repairing roads.

your condition now: if you had only unfolded your umbrella and held it over you, the sun wouldn't have made you tired. Spiritual power and spiritual qualities exist within you, but because you are not aware of them, you experience sorrow. Life cannot be blamed for this. All you need to do is get rid of the ego and install God in its place. There is no need to go anywhere in search of peace. Truth and noble ideals—that is God. But there is no room for such ideals in a mind filled with the sense of "I." The ego should be eradicated with the help of humbleness. Then, through the power within us, we will experience peace. By heating metal in a fire, we can mold it into any shape we like. Similarly, by offering our ego to the fire of God, we can transform ourselves into our true nature.

Question – Mother, can we really find inner peace through spiritual practice?

Mother – You won't find peace by doing spiritual practice alone. You also have to give up the ego. Only then will you experience the benefit from your practice and attain peace of mind. You may ask, "Does everyone who prays to God or sings devotional songs attain peace?" Only if you understand the spiritual principles and then pray or sing, will your mind become strong. Spiritual practice will benefit only those who, having studied the scriptures or listened to spiritual discourses, have gained some understanding of the spiritual principles, and who live according to those teachings. There's a story about an ascetic who turned a bird into ashes because it disturbed his spiritual practice. He had gone through many austerities, yet it took only an instant for his anger to flare up. If you perform spiritual practice without having any understanding of spirituality, and without having imbibed the teachings of any great souls, all you will have is arrogance and anger.

Question – I have prayed to most of the deities I know of. I have worshipped Shiva, Devi, and others in turn, chanting many different mantras. Still, I don't feel I have benefited from any of it.

Mother – A person was very thirsty but no water was available. Someone told her, "Dig here and you will soon find water." So she dug in that place for a little while, but didn't find any water. She started digging at another spot but didn't find any water there either. She moved to yet another spot and dug again, but there was no water. Thus she kept digging in many different places, but to no avail. She finally collapsed from exhaustion. A passerby saw her lying there and asked what had happened. She replied, "I am exhausted from digging everywhere for water. Now I am suffering more than before, because, at first, I was only thirsty; but now I have wasted all my strength digging and am also exhausted." The passerby said, "If you had only had a little patience and had continued digging deeper in just one spot, you would have found more than enough water right at the beginning. Instead, you dug a little in many different places and all you got was disappointment!" This is what the result of praying to different Gods is like. You won't benefit from it. However, if you think of all the Gods as being one and the same God when you pray to them, then there is no problem. The trouble lies in constantly shifting your focus from one form to another.

A man bought a seedling of a certain type of mango

tree, which was expected to yield fruit in three years. He planted it and cultivated it as required. But just as the tree was about to flower, he uprooted it and planted another sapling in its stead. Only two days remained to complete the three years! He didn't have the patience to wait, so how could he possibly receive any fruit? Similarly, you didn't have the patience to wait for as long as was needed, daughter. You went to many different places, chanted different mantras, and meditated on several deities. And so you didn't get any fruits. Also, you prayed to God for material prosperity, and not out of any real longing for God. Devotion aimed at gaining material success is not true devotion. Daughter, you meditated on the objects you desired, not on God. That is why you kept running around to so many places. You chanted one mantra, but when that gave no result, you took up another mantra. When that, too, failed, you turned to yet another. What came of all this? Only a waste of time!

Daughter, you wanted only the gold in the King's palace. You didn't love the King. If you had loved the King, you would have received both the gold and the King himself. If you had loved God alone, you would have gained everything.

But you did not love God. You longed only for the gold. If you had done spiritual practice, without being attached to anything; if you had given up all desires, surrendered everything to God, and had the attitude that everything is God's will, you would have been the Queen of all three worlds by now. But you wanted only material riches. Thus you became like Duryodhana. He wanted only the kingdom and power over his subjects. And what did he get?

He and his supporters lost everything. And the Pandavas? They looked upon the Lord as their sole refuge. Because of this attitude, they received both the Lord and the kingdom as well. So give up yearning for external happiness! When you have God, everything will come to you. Truly surrender everything. Do your spiritual practice with patience. Then you will definitely obtain not only the fruit but worldly riches also. It is pointless to expect immediate results after repeating your mantra for just a short while. You need to have patience and an attitude of surrender.

Question – Mother, some people say that weeping for God while praying and singing devotional songs is a weakness. They ask, "Doesn't our energy get dissipated, just as it does when we talk?"

Mother – An egg is destroyed by the heat of a fire, but it hatches from the heat of the mother hen. Although we are talking about heat in both cases, the results are quite different, aren't they? Idle talk drains our strength, while praying and singing devotional songs makes our minds one-pointed, and thus we gain strength. How can that be a sign of weakness? As a candle melts down, its flame gets brighter. Similarly, praying and singing with a melting heart takes us to the state of Supreme Truth. Crying for God is not a weakness.

Question – Mother, do we lose strength through our thoughts?

Mother – Through spiritual thoughts we gain power and cultivate strong minds. God represents all good qualities, such as self-sacrifice, love, and compassion. When we think about God, those virtues will awaken in us and our minds will expand. But when we think about material things, the mind becomes immersed in worldliness and wanders among different objects, one after the other. Our senses respond to the wandering mind; bad qualities develop in us and our minds contract. And when we fail to get what we desire, we weaken even further and get angry; we lose our strength.

Every time a lighter is used, it loses some of its energy. Similarly, whenever we talk about something that strengthens our worldly desires, our minds get weaker and our energy dissipates. On the other hand, thinking and talking about spiritual matters is like charging a battery. So, in one case we lose energy, while in the other we gain energy.

Question – It is said that a woman shouldn't go to a temple or do puja during her monthly period. Is this true? Isn't God everywhere? Surely God isn't confined to a particular place.

Mother – God is omnipresent. God is everywhere, always. But we do have to consider certain issues such as purity or impurity. External purity leads to internal purity. During a woman's menstrual period, her mind is not calm. Her body also feels tired, as it does during pregnancy. So she should rest at that time. During her period, a woman is usually not able to pray or do puja with proper concentration. But if she does have the strength and concentration, then it is fine for her to do puja.

Many changes take place in a woman's body during menstruation. There are certain bad germs in the body during this time. One of Mother's American sons refused at first to believe this when Mother said it. But when he returned to America he found out about a scientific experiment. Several women were asked to pick flowers from the same plant. Some of the women had their menstrual periods and others did not. The flowers picked by women with their periods withered faster than those picked by others. Only after he heard about this experiment, did that son believe what Mother had said.

Mother has met many people. She speaks on the basis of their experiences as well. These days, people believe something only if they read it in the newspapers. Even if someone comes and tells them that they saw a baby fall into the water, people won't believe it. They will say, "Let us see it in the newspaper; then we will believe it."

It is good if a woman continues to chant her mantra during her monthly period, but it is better not to go to any temples. Mother says this with the purity of the temple atmosphere in mind. When you visit a temple, you don't have the same attitude as you do in an office or at a restaurant. The whole concept of the temple is different, and that sanctity should be preserved.

God is like the wind. The wind blows equally over flowers and excreta. For God, there are no differences such as purity or impurity. But we still have to be aware of those differences, for only then can we progress.

Question – Mother, why do people continue to suffer after taking refuge in God? Why can't God fulfill everyone's desires?

Mother – Today most people take refuge in God only to get their wishes fulfilled. That is not love for God; it is just love for worldly objects. Because of their desires, which are rooted in selfishness, they have little compassion for anyone. How can God's grace enter into the heart of someone who feels no compassion for others? So how can such a person get rid of his or her suffering? If you pray to God only to have your wishes fulfilled, you won't find freedom from suffering. If you want your suffering to end, you have to pray for your desires to end, and for your faith and love for God to grow. Then God will fulfill all your needs. Our love shouldn't be for the trivial things in the King's palace. We should love the King Himself. Having caught the King, all the treasures in the palace will be ours. When we pray to God, it shouldn't be for a job or a house or a baby. We should pray, "God, I want You to be my very own." If we have God, if we can earn God's grace, then all three worlds will be at our feet. We will be given the power to rule over those worlds. But to achieve this, our thoughts, words, and actions have to be good.

My children, you should pray for God alone. Only then will you ever be completely fulfilled. Whatever falls into sugar becomes sweet. Similarly, because God is bliss, our closeness to God gives us bliss. If you catch the queen bee, all the other bees will follow her. If you take refuge in God, all spiritual and material gains will be yours.

The faith and devotion of those who turn to God to get their desires fulfilled will increase only for as long as their wishes are granted. When their wishes are not fulfilled, they lose whatever faith they had.

How can everyone's wishes be fulfilled? A doctor wishes to have lots of patients. So he prays for this every day. Wouldn't he lose faith if he didn't have any patients?

Meanwhile, the patients pray for health. The prayer of the undertaker is that there will be corpses to transport daily without fail, and the coffin-seller's prayer is the same. And what about others? They pray that they will never die! How can the prayers of both sides be granted? An attorney prays for lawsuits, while everyone else prays not to get involved in any lawsuits. This world contains countless such contradictions. It would be difficult for everyone's wishes to be granted simultaneously. And, yet, it isn't that hard to live in peace and contentment in this world of contradictions. We need to grasp the principles of spirituality and live accordingly, that's all.

Growing coconut trees is not difficult for a person who has studied agriculture. If the trees become infested with a disease, the person will be able to recognize it quickly and cure them. Similarly, if you are familiar with the spiritual principles and live according to those principles, you will know how to go forward in life without faltering when faced with difficulties.

When you buy a machine you get an instruction manual. If you are not familiar with the machine and start using it without reading the instructions, the machine may break down. The mahatmas and spiritual texts teach us how to live properly in this world. If we follow their teachings, our lives will be fulfilled. If we don't, our lives will be wasted.

Question – Mother, we say that God is the Source of all compassion. Why, then, does God give people terrible diseases and make them suffer?

Mother – God is not the cause of any illnesses. Nor

does God punish anyone. People's selfishness causes diseases. Think of how many countless wrongs people commit out of their selfishness! It is the consequences of this that they suffer.

People create artificial environments to increase their comforts. Chemical fertilizers are used to increase crops, and chemicals are added to get bigger and faster-growing produce. Fruits cannot give us their natural quality when we grow them through such artificial means. Nor have we excluded animals from such treatment. Plants and animals subjected to chemicals are not the only ones who suffer ill effects. Humans who eat the contaminated food also suffer.

Intoxicants also cause diseases. Intoxicants like alcohol and cannabis destroy certain elements in a man's sperm and weaken it. Many of the children born from such sperm suffer from ill health and deformities. Today's polluted atmosphere is yet another cause of ill health. Air and water are contaminated by toxic fumes and waste materials. We breathe in that polluted air and drink the contaminated water. Nothing pure is available today. And all this has been caused by the selfishness of humans. It is not God, but people's wrong actions stemming from their selfishness and unnatural behavior, that cause so many illnesses. It is pointless to blame God for this.

By its increasing selfishness, humankind is digging its own grave. People are digging where they stand and will fall into that hole. They do not realize this. Those who want twice as much of everything—whether food or wealth—are in fact stealing what belongs to others. Because of their greed, others don't have enough to meet their needs. Selfish people don't experience any peace during their lives or after they die. They are in hell while alive and will be in greater hell after they die.[24]

Nature has lost her rhythm and harmony, being permeated with the breath of selfish humans who have lost their truthfulness and loving kindness. Today when it rains, there is nothing but rain; and when the sun shines, there is nothing but sun. Farming doesn't function the way it should.

Humanity has a duty to protect nature, but who cares these days? Our present happiness is like spitting up in the air while lying on our backs. If we continue to forsake our dharma and to harm Mother Nature, the consequences will be ten times as bad as at present. But even then, people will blame God instead of trying to better themselves!

My children, real knowledge is to know the mind—to know the Self. It teaches us how to apply the divine principles in our lives. Hardly anyone tries to acquire that wisdom now. Yet, this is what we need to learn above all else.

Learn how to hunt before you go hunting, and you won't waste your arrows; nor will you be in danger of becoming prey to wild animals. If you understand how we are meant to live, your life can be truly meaningful.

If you know the route before setting out on a journey, you won't get lost and be forced to wander. Also, if you draw an architectural plan before you start building a house, the house will be constructed properly. Similarly, peace will permeate the lives of those who have acquired a real understanding of the mind. But self-centered people have

24 Mother doesn't refer to hell as an eternal state. It is a temporary state in which one has to suffer and exhaust the fruits of one's negative actions.

no interest in this. They don't care about the welfare of the world. All that is important to them is their own happiness—but they won't even experience that happiness.

My children, to really love God is to have compassion for the poor and to serve them. The whole world will kneel before those who live selflessly, who surrender their selfishness to God. When we pray, only God should be present in our hearts. No space should be allowed in our hearts for anything else. Mother has seen those who pray at the temple and then run straight to the nearest liquor shop for a drink. She has also seen people who leave every few minutes to smoke when they come to see Her. They can't even give up such meaningless little things. How, then, can they expect to attain God?

Question – Different people have different concepts about God. What is God really?

Mother – It isn't possible to describe the nature of God or His attributes. God has to be experienced. Can we with words convey the taste of honey or the beauty of nature? Only by tasting and seeing can we know the qualities of such things. God is beyond words, beyond all limitations. God is everywhere and in everyone. God is present in all that is sentient and insentient. We cannot say that God has a particular form. Nor can we say that God is precisely this or that. What we call Brahman is the same as God. Brahman permeates every space of which we can possibly conceive and beyond.

Question – But, to think about God, don't we have to have a concept?

Mother – God is beyond all attributes. One cannot describe God. But to help our minds to comprehend God, we say that God has certain qualities. Those qualities are reflected in selfless mahatmas such as Sri Rama and Sri Krishna. God's qualities include truthfulness, dharma, self-sacrifice, love, and compassion. Those qualities are God. When those qualities develop in us, we come to know the nature of God. But only if we let go of our egos will those qualities be reflected in us. Though the fruits and flowers are contained within the seed, the seed has to go beneath the soil, and its shell (the ego) has to break before the fruits and flowers can emerge. When the shell breaks and the seedling grows into a tree, everyone will benefit. A tree continues to give us shade even while we are cutting it down.

When your renunciation is such that your heart becomes like a mirror, you will know God's form and experience His beauty. God's attributes will then be reflected in you.

Question – What about the saying that God is devoid of attributes?

Mother – God is attributeless. But ordinary people require an upadhi (a means, tool or symbol) to grasp God. Suppose you are thirsty and need water. You will need a container to hold the water. When you have drunk the water you can discard the container. It is very difficult to comprehend God as nirguna (without attributes). God therefore assumes the form in which the devotee has visualized

Him. This aspect of God with attributes is easier for us to absorb. Just like a ladder that helps you to climb a tree, the upadhi helps you to reach the goal.

Also, a person who can't climb a tree can still pick mangos if he has a long pole with a hook attached to it. Similarly, we need a tool to help bring out the good qualities within us. It is through such tools or symbols that the power of God manifests. In reality, God is attributeless. Suppose you mold a piece of chocolate into a certain shape. There is now a form to see. But expose it to heat and it will melt. There will no longer be a form.

Question – It is said that God resides in our hearts. Is this true?

Mother – How can we say that God, who is all-powerful and all-pervading, resides within anything in particular? Imagine if you were to try to squeeze a big bag into a tiny glass. The bag would remain mostly outside the glass, hiding the glass from view. If you dip a pitcher in a river, there will be water both inside and outside the pitcher. Similarly, God cannot be confined within any form. God is beyond all forms. So how is it possible to have any real concept about God, who is beyond all symbols, beyond all limitations? For our own convenience, to help us visualize God, we refer to something as God's abode. There are those who believe that God resides in the heart. For them, God is in the heart. For someone else who believes that God dwells in a certain building, God is in that building. It all depends on each person's imagination. When Mira was given poison and considered it God's prasad (gift of grace), it ceased to be poison. Prahlada saw God everywhere, even in a pillar and in a piece of straw. Those who fully understand that God is all-pervasive will really experience God. Those who do not have that faith can never realize God.

Question – Why is it said that among living beings God is reflected most clearly in humans?

Mother – Only humans have the power of discrimination. When a moth sees fire, it thinks it is food; it flies into it and perishes. But a human being uses his or her discrimination. Humans were aware of the usefulness of fire and learned to cook food with it. They used it to create light in the dark. For those who have the power of discrimination, fire is useful. For others, it is dangerous. Fire is useful to a human, but death to a moth. Thus there is a good and bad side to everything in the universe. Those who recognize the good side in everything truly understand the principle of God. Such beings can only benefit the world.

Question – Mother, what is meant by moksha (liberation)?

Mother – Everlasting bliss is known as liberation. This can be experienced here on earth. Heaven and hell exist here on earth. If we do only good deeds, we will be happy after death as well.

Those who are aware of the Self enjoy the state of bliss at every moment. They find that bliss within themselves. They experience it in their every action. They are the courageous ones. They do only good and are not worried about life or death. They are not concerned about any suffering that may come to them or about being harmed by anyone. Wherever they are, they live in accordance with truth.

If you put a renunciate in prison, he or she will find joy even there. Such people see God in the actions of everyone. A prison cannot bind them. They never complain about anyone. During each moment they live with awareness of the Self.

As long as a frog is still a tadpole with a tail, it can live only in water. When the tail disappears, the frog can live both in water and on land. You cannot be free of samsara (the cycle of birth, death, and rebirth) until you lose your tail, i.e., the ego. When you lose that tail, you will be in bliss whether you stay in your body or leave it.

A rubber ball will float if it falls into water. It has no problem on land either. It isn't bound by anything. Likewise, the nature of those who live in a state of Self-awareness is special. Night and day are the same for them. Their bliss lies within themselves, not in any external objects. Liberation consists of this mental attitude.

If you are born in a body, you are bound to experience both happiness and sorrow, for that is the nature of life. Happiness and sorrow interchange according to your actions. Coolness is the nature of water and heat the nature of fire. It is the nature of a river to flow. The river keeps flowing; it doesn't stop permanently anywhere. Similarly, happiness and sorrow are the nature of life. If you understand this, you can cheerfully accept both pleasure and suffering when they come your way. Those who do this are not affected by any of the obstacles that arise from this world. They are always blissful. And that is liberation.

Two travelers spent the night in an inn beside a pond. For one of them, staying there was unbearable because of the sound of the frogs and crickets. Seeing the man's discomfort, his companion said, "Frogs and crickets make noises at night; that's their nature. We cannot change their inborn traits. So why let it bother you? Let us go to bed." And having said that, he went to sleep. But the other man couldn't sleep. He left the inn and went looking for a quieter place to stay. But he couldn't sleep anywhere, because wherever he went there was always some noise that disturbed him. His friend who ignored the noise, knowing it is the nature of frogs and crickets to croak and chirp, had no trouble sleeping. Similarly, when we understand that whatever others say is due to their nature, there is no need for us to feel unhappy about it. If we can develop this attitude, we can happily overcome any obstacles.

Today people do not experience peace within themselves because of the conflicts in their minds. To avoid such conflicts, you have to attain knowledge of the mind, which is spiritual knowledge. It is not difficult for someone who has studied agriculture to plant and cultivate trees or to treat a sick tree. But if you try to plant trees without knowing anything about the subject, nine out of ten of the trees you plant will probably die. Similarly, if you understand what life is really about, your life will not be wasted. So, obtain spiritual knowledge; then you will experience liberation both here on earth and after death.

If you know the way when you're traveling, you won't waste time. Otherwise, it will take you much longer to get there. If you are lost and wandering about, you won't experience any peace of mind; you will constantly worry about whether or not you will reach your destination. It is best to travel with full knowledge of the route, for then your journey will be calm and pleasant.

Long ago spiritual wisdom was taught at the gurukulas, along with worldly knowledge. Those who received spiritual training had no mental conflicts or lack of inner peace. Even those who associated with them experienced peace. Those people had no greed. They were free from illusions. But today the situation is quite different. People have learned how to air-condition the outer environment, but they don't know how to "air-condition" their minds. They can't sleep even in their air-conditioned rooms. They need pills, alcohol, or drugs to help them forget their troubles. When you possess spiritual knowledge and wisdom, there is no need for any of that. Your mind will be at peace always, whether you happen to be in a hut or in a palace, because that wisdom is the understanding of the mind.

If you wish to experience peace without end, you need to have an understanding of what is everlasting and what is fleeting. A pet snake is given milk even though it could bite. We should remember that it is a snake we are feeding, because it is bound to show its true nature. If we understand people's true nature when we are dealing with them, we won't end up being disappointed. As we deal with the world, we should be aware of its true nature.

A bank manager knows that the money under his responsibility is not his own. He is therefore not bothered about giving hundreds of thousands of rupees to others. He knows his duty is to take care of the money. Many people approach him for loans. They offer him all sorts of things and act very loving and polite. But that is not real love.

Those people are not really his friends. He knows they wouldn't hesitate to falsely accuse him and have him sent to jail if it would benefit them. This is the nature of people's love. If they show any love, it is only for the sake of their own happiness. They would even destroy our lives if it were to their advantage. God is the only real family we have. The Self is our only friend. If we grasp this truth in life, we won't have any problems. We will be able to travel the path to liberation. Freedom from all attachments—that is liberation. So, perform all your actions as your duty, without having any expectations of liberation. Just keep your mind focused on God.

Question – Mother, what is maya?

Mother – Whatever doesn't give you lasting peace, that is maya (illusion). None of the things we perceive through our senses can give us peace. They can only make us suffer. In truth they are nonexistent, just like dreams.

A poor man won a fortune in a lottery. With the help of his newfound wealth, he married the beautiful princess of the land and was given half the kingdom as well. One day he and the princess went out riding together on a mountain. Suddenly a very strong wind blew up and the horses and riders fell down the mountain. The princess and the horses were killed, but the man managed to hold on to a tree branch and survive. Safe ground lay just beneath him. He closed his eyes and jumped. But when he opened his eyes, there was no mountain, no princess, no horses and no palace! There were only the walls and mud floor of his hut. He had been starving for two days, had collapsed out of hunger and exhaustion, and had fallen asleep. And now as he awakened, he realized that everything he had seen was only a dream. He did not grieve for the loss of the princess or the kingdom, because he knew it had all been a dream.

During the dream, everything was real. Only if you awaken from the dream you are in now, will you know Reality.

Those who live close to a cremation ground are not afraid to live there or to walk through the area. For them, it is only a place where corpses are burned. But others not living there are afraid to walk through that area, because, to them, it is a haunted place. If they were to walk there at night and happened to stumble on a stone or see a leaf moving in the wind, they would tremble with fear. Whatever they set their eyes on would turn into a ghost. If they were to see a pillar, they'd mistake it for a ghost and would faint. Similarly, people destroy themselves because of their mistaken projections onto every object.

A person walking through a forest inhabited by snakes will scream with fear if he happens to be pricked by a thorn. He will assume that a snake bit him. He will even exhibit all the symptoms of a snakebite until a doctor arrives and explains that he hasn't been bitten at all. Many people have these sorts of experiences. They lose their strength focusing on what doesn't exist. This is how people live today because of their inability to see the truth.

For this reason we shouldn't be attached to material objects. Those who are attached to things will experience only suffering. This is why it is all known as maya (illusion). If we look upon everything as the essence of Divinity, we won't have to experience suffering; there will be only happiness.

Question – Is this universe maya?

Mother – Yes, the universe is indeed an illusion. Those who get caught in the illusion experience only obstacles and suffering. When you are able to distinguish between the eternal and the transient, you will clearly see that it is all an illusion. We say that the universe is maya. But if we choose only what is positive in our lives, we will not be bound by the illusion. This will help us to progress on the right path.

Let us say you are out walking on a muddy ridge between two rice fields, and you slip and fall in the mud. You are covered with mud. To you, the mud is dirt that you want to wash off. But a potter walking that same way sees the mud as something useful. To him, the mud is an excellent type of clay, and he proceeds to use it for his work. To the potter, the mud isn't dirt at all.

A woman gathering firewood in a forest comes across a stone. Thinking it is just the right shape, she uses it as a grinding stone. Another person, who knows a lot about stones, sees that same stone and recognizes it as a stone of special quality. He installs the stone in a temple as a divine image. He offers fruits and gems to the deity and worships it. But to those who do not understand its greatness, it is just a stone.

You can cook your food on a fire. You can also burn your house down with that same fire. You can sew with a needle. You can also injure your eye with it. To a doctor, a scalpel is an instrument used for surgery to save a patient. To the murderer, it is a lethal weapon. So, rather than dismiss everything as maya, we should consider the real place for each object and use it accordingly. The negative side of things should be dismissed. The great sages saw only goodness in everything in the universe.

Those who are fully aware of maya do not succumb to it. They protect the world. On the other hand, those who don't understand maya not only destroy themselves but also become a burden to others. They are committing a form of suicide. If you go through life accepting only the good side of everything, you won't view anything as an illusion. Everything has the potential to lead us to goodness.

A dog sees the moon reflected in a pool of water and jumps barking into the water. The dog doesn't look up at the real moon. A child jumps into a well to catch the moon and drowns. The dog and the child are not aware of reality. Both the everlasting and the transitory exist, but we have to distinguish between them. What is the use of trying to catch the shadow while ignoring the real thing? The shadow, maya, lasts only for as long as "I" (the ego) lasts. Where there is no "I", there is no universe, no illusion.

Because our knowledge is incomplete, we think the illusion is real. There is no shadow at noon when the sun reaches its zenith. Having reached the zenith of knowledge (enlightenment), we will see only Reality.

Question – It is said that we experience that the universe exists only because of maya (illusion). Then, why does it seem so utterly real?

Mother – Creation exists only when there is a notion of "I." Without that notion, there is no creation, there are no living beings. Only Brahman remains forever Brahman.

A child wants a doll so much that she cries for several hours. She finally gets a doll and plays with it for some time. She won't allow anyone else to touch it. She goes to sleep clasping the doll close to her. But now, as she sleeps, the doll slips to the floor, and the child isn't even aware of it.

A man hides his gold beneath his pillow and goes to sleep with his head resting on the pillow. But while he sleeps, a thief comes and steals it all. When he was awake, the man could think of nothing but his gold, and because of that he had no peace. But in his sleep he forgot everything; he wasn't aware of himself or his family or his possessions. There was only bliss. The bliss we experience in deep sleep is what gives us the energy we feel when we wake up. Once we wake up, "my doll," "my necklace," and "my family" all come back. As the sense of "I" returns, everything else returns along with it.

Brahman exists as Brahman—always. But we will experience Brahman only when our thoughts subside.

Question – Mother, if everyone were to lead a spiritual life and become sannyasis, how would the world survive? What is the benefit of sannyasa?

Mother – Not everyone can become a sannyasi. Out of a million people who try, only a few will succeed. But just because everyone can't get a medical degree or secure a high job position, it doesn't mean that one should give up trying.

Mother isn't saying that everyone should become a

sannyasi, but if you understand the principle behind sannyasa and live accordingly, you can avoid suffering. Then you will be able to overcome any obstacles with detachment.

What Mother means is that we should give up the sense of "I" and "mine." Whatever we wish for, we should understand its role in life. Also, our actions shouldn't be performed with any expectation of their fruits, because expectation is the cause of suffering.

A person on a fund-raising drive went to a house to collect a contribution. He expected at least a thousand rupees, but the family gave him only five! He was furious and refused to accept the donation. He was still angry a year later! He nursed his anger inside. Because he hadn't received what he expected, he wasn't able to accept what was offered. He rejected it because he was so disappointed. If he hadn't held any expectations, he wouldn't have had to go through all that anger and suffering. He would have been satisfied with what little he received. We can avoid this sort of suffering on our journey through life, if we are like beggars. A beggar knows he is a beggar, so he doesn't grieve if he isn't given anything. He isn't sad if he doesn't receive anything in one place, because he knows he will perhaps get something in the next place. He knows that being given a whole armful or being left empty-handed are both part of his experience on the journey through life. So he doesn't feel angry with anyone. When you are a true beggar, you look upon everything as God's will. Let your bond be with God—that is all Mother is saying. The truly spiritual ones have no sorrows.

Today people are attached to external things. "That's my family"—this is how they go through life, and it is for their family they toil day and night without rest. But they forget themselves. They fail to discover their dharma and to live accordingly. They forget God. When you live in this way, you do not find peace in life, nor after death.

This doesn't mean that we shouldn't work. We should perform our actions, but without harboring any expectations or desires.

Happiness is not to be found in outward things. Happiness lies within ourselves.

When you have eaten a large portion of your favorite sweet dish, you won't feel like eating any more of it—you would begin to hate it if you did. If someone were to place another portion in front of you, you would push it away. If it were really the sweet dish that had made you happy, would there be any reason to push it away? Wouldn't you eat more of it? So, the mind is the cause here. When the mind is satiated, we begin to dislike the object. Everything depends on the mind. Happiness is not somewhere on the outside; it is within you. So search for it there! If you go in search of happiness outside of yourself—in your relationships with people and in external objects—your life will be wasted. This doesn't mean that you should sit idly doing nothing. Whenever possible, do something for others. Serve those in need. Repeat a mantra. Live your life dedicated to the spiritual goal.

Question – Mother, how can we eliminate worldly vasanas (latent tendencies)?

Mother – You can't just pick up and remove a vasana any more than you can pick up a bubble out of water. The bubble will break if you try to take it out. Bubbles arise because of the waves in the water. To avoid bubbles, we have to be watchful so that waves don't arise. Through positive thoughts and contemplation we reduce the waves that arise in the mind from worldly vasanas. There is no room for worldly vasanas in a mind quieted through positive thoughts.

Question – It is said that the objects enjoyed through our senses cannot give us happiness. But, still, it is really from material objects that I derive happiness, isn't it?

Mother – Happiness doesn't come from outside of yourself. Some people adore chocolate, but no matter how delicious it is, when you have eaten ten pieces at once, you will begin to feel an aversion to chocolate. You won't get the same satisfaction from the eleventh piece as you got from the first. Some people don't like chocolate at all. Just the smell of it makes them nauseated. But chocolate always remains the same, whether or not people like it. If the chocolate really made us happy, wouldn't we feel equally happy regardless of how much we ate? And wouldn't everyone derive satisfaction from it? So our satisfaction doesn't depend on the chocolate per se, but on our minds. People believe they derive happiness externally and spend their entire lives trying to acquire the objects of their desires. But in the end the senses die, we become feeble, and collapse.

Happiness is to be found within, not without. Only if we rely on that inner happiness can we enjoy bliss and satisfaction always. Both material objects and the senses that perceive them have limitations. It is not that the materialistic aspect of life should be avoided; only that we should understand the intended use of each object and give it only the importance it deserves in our lives. Unnecessary thoughts and expectations are the problem.

For most people, nothing is more important than their own happiness. They don't love anyone beyond that. A man came to see Mother in America. His wife had died recently. She was his life. When she was away, he would stay up all night, sleepless. He wouldn't eat if she hadn't eaten. Whenever she went somewhere, he would wait for her. He adored his wife. But their life together didn't last long. She suddenly contracted a minor illness and died within a week. The body was taken to the funeral parlor. Many friends and relatives arrived. The burial was to take place only after everyone had viewed the body. Meanwhile, the husband became very hungry. "Oh, let it be over soon!" he said to himself. He wanted it to finish so that he could eat. He waited for another hour or two. Still, he saw no sign of the burial taking place any time soon. By this time he was so hungry that he went to a nearby restaurant and ordered a meal. He himself told Mother about this incident. He said, "Mother, I was willing to sacrifice my life for my wife—I loved her that much. But I forgot everything when I was hungry!"

This happened in America. Now don't you want to hear what happened in India? This is the story told by a woman who came to the ashram. Her husband was killed by a car while he was riding a bicycle. This woman was his second wife. The first wife had died some years earlier. There were two grownup children from that first marriage. When the second wife received the news of her husband's death, the first thing she did was not to go and see the body or to bring it home; instead she went to take possession of the key to her husband's safe. By the time she found the key, some people arrived with the body. The children of the first wife also arrived. After hearing about their father's death, they didn't immediately go to see his body. They, too, went straight to the place where he kept the key to the safe. They wanted to find the key before their stepmother found it, because they feared she would take all of their father's wealth. But they arrived too late. The stepmother had already found the key and hidden it. Those children had been raised with so much love. Where was their love now? The wife used to say that she loved her husband more than her own life. Where was her love now? Their minds were only on the money. My children, this is what the world is like. People tend to love others only out of selfish motives.

Some men vow to kill their wife if she talks to another man. When a father is on his deathbed, the son can't wait to divide the property. In some cases, if the son expects to receive a big inheritance, he won't hesitate to take his father's life. Is that love?

The point is not that we should give up and just sit idly, not doing any work, because the world is the way it is. But we shouldn't have any expectations such as "My wife or husband and my children will stay with me forever."

Know your dharma, and strive to live accordingly. Perform your actions without any expectations. Don't expect love, wealth, fame, or anything else. The aim of our actions should be to purify our inner selves. Be attached only to what is spiritual, for only then will you experience true happiness.

If you perform certain actions expecting something from others, suffering will be your only companion. But if you live in harmony with the spiritual principles, you will be in heaven here on earth and in heaven when you die. You will benefit both yourself and the world.

Question – The Self has no form. How, then, can we recognize its influence?

Mother – Air is formless, but if you put it in a balloon, you can play with it, tossing it up and about. Likewise, the Self is formless and all-pervading. We can understand its influence with the help of an upadhi (the means through which the Infinite expresses itself in the manifest world).

Question – Is it possible for a person to always be in a state of non-duality? Isn't it only in samadhi that it becomes possible? Doesn't the person return to the world of duality when he or she "wakes up" from samadhi?

Mother – From your viewpoint the person exists in a state of duality, but he or she is still in that non-dualistic, direct experience of Reality. Once you have mixed rice flour and sugar together, you can't separate them, and only sweetness remains. Similarly, once you reach the state of non-duality—at the level of direct experience—you are that. Then, there is no duality in your world; you view everything you do in the light of your non-dual experience.

A fully enlightened being is like a burned lime peel or a burned rope: it appears to have a certain form, but the form vanishes the moment you touch it. The actions of an enlightened being appear to be like the actions of ordinary people, but the enlightened one revels in the Self always. He or she is verily the Self.

Question – Could you give some sort of description of the non-dual experience?

Mother – That is beyond words. You cannot taste sugar and explain exactly how sweet it is. It is indescribable. When you eat food, you see the benefit afterwards, don't you? The benefit of sleep is the energy and peace you feel when you wake up. The profound, ineffable peace experienced during samadhi remains even after coming out of that state.

Question – Some people are born rich. They grow up in the midst of plenty. Others are born in huts where there is not enough for even a single meal. What is the reason for this difference?

Mother – Each person is reborn in accordance with the actions of his or her previous lives. Some people are born under kesari yoga[25] and will prosper anywhere. The Goddess of prosperity resides in them. In accordance with the actions of their previous lives, they have been born now with this deity. In their previous lives, they have worshipped God with concentration and given generously to others. Those who have done bad deeds are the ones who suffer now.

Question – But we are not aware of any of this.

Mother – Can you remember everything you did as a

25 In astrology, kesari yoga is a special configuration of the moon and Jupiter at the time of a person's birth, which indicates a very auspicious and prosperous future.

child? During their exams don't students often forget what they studied the day before? Similarly, everything has been forgotten. And yet, with the eye of wisdom, we can see everything.

Question – How can we be released from suffering?

Mother – Those who truly absorb spirituality and live according to dharma do not experience sorrow. What is the use of just sitting and crying if your hand is cut? You have to apply a salve to the wound. If you just sit and cry, the wound could become infected and you could even die.

Suppose someone verbally abuses you and you react by sitting in a corner crying. You are unhappy because you accepted the abuse. If you don't accept it, it becomes that person's problem, not yours. So you have to disown it. If you act with discrimination in this way, you will attain freedom from suffering.

Again, if your hand is cut, what is the use of pausing and analyzing how it happened—what type of knife caused the cut and so on—without taking care of the wound?

If a person is bitten by a poisonous snake and just sits there, brooding about the snake, death will come. Or, let's say that someone receives a snakebite. She rushes home, opens the encyclopedia and tries to figure out what remedy to take. She will die before she finally discovers that she needs a serum. When someone is bitten by a snake, a serum is needed as quickly as possible.

When suffering comes our way, we should try to overcome it, rather than weaken at the thought of it. Certain sages of old learned the essential truths and applied them in their lives. If we heed their words and live according to the scriptural guidelines, we can move through any situation without faltering. Spiritual knowledge is far more essential in life than worldly knowledge, for it teaches us how to live in this world. For as long as we don't apply that wisdom in our lives, it is toward hell that we journey, both in this life and hereafter.

Gurukulas teach people this spiritual wisdom—how to experience peace in this world, how to lead a life without hardships. The spiritual masters are the doctors of the mind.

Question – Aren't psychiatrists the doctors of the mind?

Mother – They treat the mind only when it loses its balance. A spiritual master teaches us how to live in order to avoid any of that. This is what gurukulas are for.

Question – It is said that desires are the cause of suffering. By which method can we get rid of our desires?

Mother – Would we deliberately allow a person who wishes to hurt us to live with us? Would we want to sleep anywhere near a dangerous madman? No—because we know the madman's mind is unstable and that he could harm us. Similarly, if we bring up a snake, no matter what we feed it, the snake will inevitably show its true nature. And no one would want to keep a rabid dog at home. If our dog is infected with rabies, we won't hesitate to have it put to sleep, even though the dog is very dear to us. We try to avoid such creatures, knowing that associating with them causes suffering.

If we study the nature of everything in this way, and accept only what is beneficial, we won't have to experience suffering.

Desires can never take us to perfection. Failing to understand this, people nurture their negative desires. Thus they have to face many problems and they cause others to suffer as well. Would you deliberately drink poison? Even if you are very hungry, if a poisonous spider falls into your food, you won't touch the food. Similarly, once you fully understand that your desire for material objects causes suffering, your mind will no longer be drawn to those objects. Thus, if you go through life with alertness, you can be free from desires. This is very difficult. Nevertheless, with enough alertness, discrimination, detachment, contemplation, and practice, it is possible.

Question – We are told that there are many mahatmas endowed with divine power now living in India. It is believed that nothing is impossible for them. When people suffer hardships and die because of floods, droughts, and earthquakes, why don't the mahatmas save them?

Mother – My children, in the world of a mahatma, there is no birth or death, happiness or sorrow. If people suffer, it is due to their prarabdha (fruits of their actions in this life and former lives). They are experiencing the fruits of their karma, which they have to exhaust. It is true that the amount of one's prarabdha can be reduced by the grace of a mahatma. But one has to be fit to receive that grace. The mahatmas exist, but people don't take advantage of their presence the way they should. An arrow can hit the target only if you draw the bow before you shoot. The mahatmas show us the proper way. Why blame the mahatmas if we do not heed their advice?

So many people are born on this earth. Accordingly,

they have to die as well, don't they? But death exists for the body only, not for the soul. We came from dust; we go back to dust. The clay says to the potter, "You are making pots out of me now, but tomorrow I will make pots out of you!" Everyone gets the fruits of his or her karma.

My children, only where there is a sense of "I" can there be death. Those with a sense of "I" live only for a certain amount of years. But there is a world beyond that where there is only bliss. To reach that world, we have to make the best possible use of the life we have been given now.

For most people, being preoccupied with the concept that the world is unreal is not advisable. They should focus on developing positive qualities through good deeds. Then they will reach the "bliss bazaar" (abundance of bliss) and stay there permanently.

Question – Why did God create a planet like this one with living beings on it?

Mother – God has not created anyone. This is our creation.

A watchman guarded a storeroom containing gold and jewels. But during the night he accidentally fell asleep. Seizing the opportunity, some thieves stole everything in the storeroom. The watchman discovered the robbery upon waking up. In the throes of anxiety, he wailed, "Oh, no! What have I done! I'm going to lose my job! I won't be able to support my children!" But no such thoughts existed while he slept. During sleep he wasn't aware of any gold or thieves or of his employers. Only upon waking up did everything appear. So all of it was his own creation.

Creation came into being because of our ignorance. If one person makes a mistake, does everyone else have to imitate it? If one individual turns into a thief, does everyone else also have to steal? At any rate, if you steal you will be punished.

Let us try to remove our ignorance as soon as possible. This human life is a blessing we have received to be used for that purpose. If a cardamom plant comes up where sesame seeds were planted, what should we plant there next, sesame or cardamom? Cardamom is much more valuable than sesame seeds.

So, at least from now on, let us make room in our minds for the eternal Self. Then certain circumstances that will help us to know the Self will arise. We will enjoy bliss and go through life full of energy. Otherwise, if we insist on planting only the cheaper seeds, we will remain in poverty forever.

Question – Is it right for people to join the ashram when they have parents who will have to be looked after one day? Isn't that selfish? Who will care for the parents in their old age?

Mother – Aren't there plenty of people who don't have children? Who looks after them in their old age? It is to look after countless people that a young man or woman joins the ashram. Which is selfishness—sacrificing your life to your parents or dedicating your life to the whole world? A young person may have to leave his family and go to a different state to get a medical degree. When he returns from his studies he will be able to take care of many people. But what if he doesn't go to medical school because he feels he shouldn't leave his parents? He won't be able to save his parents from death when their time comes anyway. If he returns with a medical degree, he will at least be able to help them during times of illness.

People join the ashram to gain the strength through spiritual practice to live a life of service to the world. They show not only their parents but the whole world the right path. The path they show others by their example is one of total deliverance from suffering. But they have to control their minds to succeed in this; they have to let go of all attachments. Later they will be able to love and serve everyone. Their every breath will be for the welfare of the world.

Question – What is the reason for saying that even if something is true, it shouldn't be told if it causes pain?

Mother – There are two subjects that are spoken about in spirituality: truth and secrecy. There is nothing higher than the truth; it should never be forsaken. But all truths are not to be told openly to everyone. You have to look at the circumstances and determine whether it is necessary to reveal something. There may be occasions when something has to be kept secret even if it represents the truth. Take the example of a woman who has committed an error in a weak moment. If the world comes to know about it, her future will be ruined; her life may be in danger. But if her mistake is kept secret, she may avoid repeating it and be able to lead a positive life. In this case, it is best to keep the truth a secret, rather than reveal it. In this way it is possible to save the person's life and protect her family. But one should carefully weigh the situation before such a decision is made.

However, this should never encourage anyone to repeat a mistake. The important thing is that what we say will benefit everyone. If something we might say could cause someone pain, we shouldn't say it even if it is the truth.

Mother will give you an example. A child dies in a car accident. The accident happened a hundred kilometers away from home. It is going to be a terrible loss for the mother; this was her only child. If someone just phones her and tells her that her child is dead, she could die of shock and a broken heart. So, she is given the following phone message: "Your child was involved in a minor accident and is now in a hospital here. Please come quickly!" Even though it isn't true, saying this will enable her to hold on through that hundred kilometer journey. She will be spared the intense grief at least during that time. Once she gets there she will find out what actually happened.

Being told the truth later, after she has been told about the accident and has had time to absorb it, may lessen the effect of the shock. In this case we could be saving the mother's life by hiding the truth temporarily. The dead child is gone anyway. Is there any reason to send yet another person to her death in the name of the one who has died? These are the sort of situations Mother is talking about. Mother doesn't mean that you should tell lies.

A man with a weak heart contracts a serious illness. If he comes to know of it unexpectedly, he could have a heart attack. So the doctor doesn't break the news to him immediately. He will say only, "It isn't anything serious. You just need to rest and take this medicine." This cannot be considered an ordinary lie. The doctor doesn't say this for his own selfish gain; he is keeping a certain fact secret for the time being for the welfare of someone else.

Mother is reminded of a story. A wealthy man lived in a certain village. He used to give most of his profits to the poor. Many people would come to him for help. He knew quite a lot about spiritual matters. He used to say, "I cannot do spiritual practice all the time. I have very little time for japa and meditation. I therefore give the profits from my business to the poor, so that they will be benefited. Serving the poor is my way of worshipping God. This gives me the happiness and contentment I need. My business also prospers."

In a village some distance away lived a very poor man. He set out one day to seek the rich man's help. His family had been starving for days and he was desperate to receive whatever help he could get. But he was so weak from hunger that he could hardly walk. After covering a short distance, he felt dizzy and collapsed on the road. He was in a state of misery. He thought, "O God, I set out hoping to get some help, and look at me now, lying on this public road! I'll probably die here." He looked to one side and saw a stream beside the road. He somehow managed to get up and make his way to the water. He drank from the stream and noticed that the water was exceptionally sweet. He drank deeply and felt refreshed. The water was lovely. He fashioned a bowl out of a large leaf and collected some water in it. He felt a little stronger and slowly resumed his journey, carrying the little bowl. Finally he reached the rich man's home. There he joined a long line of people who had come to receive the gifts that were being handed out. Most of them had brought something to offer the rich man in return. Our man thought, "Oh, no! I am the only one who hasn't brought anything to give him. No matter, I will offer him this wonderful water."

So when his turn came, he offered the leaf-bowl with water to the wealthy man. The man drank a mouthful and showed his pleasure saying, "Oh, how delicious! How blessed this water is!" This made the poor man very happy. The rich man's assistants standing nearby expressed a desire to taste a little of the water, but he wouldn't allow them to do so. He put the water aside saying, "This is very sacred." He gave the poor man everything he needed and sent him on his way. Then those who were present said to the rich man, "You show no hesitation in sharing with others everything you have. Why, then, did you refuse to let us taste that holy water?" The rich man replied, "Please forgive me. That man was exhausted and drank the water he found somewhere along the way. Because of his exhaustion, the water tasted very good to him. He thought there was something special about it. That is why he brought it here. Actually, it was not fit to drink. But when I tasted it, had I said in front of him that the water was bad, that poor man would have felt hurt. Then whatever I would have given him wouldn't really have satisfied him because he would have felt so unhappy. It was because I didn't want to hurt him that I praised the water in his presence."

My children, it is in situations like this that we shouldn't tell the truth if it could hurt someone. Again, it doesn't mean that we should tell lies.

A spiritual person should never tell a lie for his or her

own sake. Our words and deeds shouldn't make a single person suffer. There is only one thing that remains without ever fading, that provides our lives with light, and that is love. My children, that love is God.

Question – If God and guru are within us, what is the need for an external guru?

Mother – A potential image lies dormant in every stone. The image can take shape only when a sculptor chisels away the unwanted parts. Similarly, the spiritual master brings out the true nature of the disciple, who, being caught in illusion, is in a state of deep forgetfulness. As long as we are unable to awaken from the illusion by ourselves, an external master is necessary. The master will remove our forgetfulness.

A student studied hard for a class. But when the teacher called on her in class, she was so nervous that her mind went blank and she couldn't remember anything. A classmate who was sitting next to her reminded her of the first line of a poem, and suddenly the whole poem sprang back into her memory. She recited the poem flawlessly for the class. Likewise, the knowledge of the Truth lies dormant within us. The master's words have the power to awaken that knowledge.

When you, as a disciple, do spiritual practice in the proximity of a master, that which is unreal in you dissolves and your real being begins to shine forth. When an image covered in wax is brought close to a fire, the wax melts and the image becomes visible. Just because a few rare individuals who realized the truth did not have a spiritual master, we cannot say that no one needs a master.

God and the spiritual master are within us in seed form. It requires a suitable climate for the seed to grow into a tree; it won't grow just anywhere. Similarly, for the innate Divinity to shine forth within us, we need a congenial environment. The master is the one who creates that environment.

Apples grow abundantly in Kashmir. The climate there is particularly favorable for apple trees. It is possible to grow apple trees in Kerala, but they require very careful cultivation; and even then, most of the saplings will wither. Because the climate in Kerala is not suitable for apple trees, the trees that do manage to survive will only give a scanty yield. Just as the climate in Kashmir is suitable for growing apples, the presence of a Self-realized master is helpful for the spiritual growth of the disciple. The master creates a suitable atmosphere for awakening the inner guru that lies dormant in the disciple, so that the disciple realizes his or her true Self.

Being practical has its place in spirituality just as it has in worldly matters. The mother holds the milk bottle for the baby and she dresses the baby. Gradually, the child learns to do these things by himself. Until people are able to do things by themselves, they need the help of others.

People who undertake a journey with the help of a map may nevertheless lose their way and wander about. But if they have a guide, they won't get lost. If there is somebody with you who knows the way, the journey will be smooth and easy. Even though the Supreme Being is within all of us, as long as we are caught in body-consciousness, we need a spiritual master. Once the aspirant has given up his or her identification with the instruments of body and mind, there is no longer a need for external guidance, for then God and the guru within have awakened.

A spiritual master is a tapasvi (someone who has undergone intense austerities). If an ordinary person is like a candle, one who does tapas (austerities) is like the sun in comparison.

However much we may dig in certain places, we will not necessarily find water. On the other hand, if we dig beside a river we can easily get water; we won't have to dig very deep. Similarly, the proximity of a true master makes the task easier for you as a disciple. You will be able to enjoy the fruits of your spiritual practice without much effort. The intensity of your prarabdha (the fruit of past actions) and the effort you need to put forth will also be lessened in the presence of a master.

Modern science admits that if we fix the mind on a point we can conserve mental strength. If this is so, how much power will there be in a yogi who has spent years practicing concentration through meditation and other spiritual practices! That is the logic behind the statement that by the mere touch of a yogi spiritual power is transmitted to others, like an electric current. A perfect master is capable not only of creating a congenial atmosphere for the spiritual progress of the disciple, but also of transmitting spiritual power to the disciple.

Only someone who has passed through the different stages of spiritual practice can properly guide a seeker.

Through reading, students can master the theory by themselves, but to be successful in the practical examination, they require the help of a teacher. Though we can learn about spirituality from books to a certain extent, in order to translate those spiritual teachings into practice, we have to seek the aid of a living master. Aspirants will come across countless obstacles and will face many problems on the spiritual path. If these problems aren't properly handled, there is a risk that the aspirants may lose their mental balance. While giving a seeker advice it is necessary to take the seeker's physical, mental, and intellectual constitution into account. Only a true master can do that. A health tonic is meant to nurture your body, but if it is consumed indiscriminately, it could do more harm than good. It is the same with spiritual practice. So, the guidance of a spiritual master is absolutely essential for a seeker.

Question – Is it possible to reach the goal solely by studying spiritual texts, without the aid of yamas and niyamas (the do's and don'ts on the spiritual path), meditation, selfless service, etc?

Mother – By studying the scriptures we are able to understand the way to God. We can learn the principles of the Self. However, merely knowing about the ways and means will not take us to the goal. To reach the goal we have to follow the path that is indicated.

Say that a man is in need of a certain object. He inquires about it and learns that it is available at a distant place. From a map he learns the way and the exact location of the place where the object is to be found. But he will not get the object unless he actually goes there and fetches it.

Or say that a woman wants to buy some medicine. The pharmacy is on the other side of a lake. So she gets into a boat, but when she reaches the other shore, she refuses to leave the boat. She just sits there and doesn't go to the pharmacy to get the medicine. That is what some people are like. They are not inclined to leave one spot along the path. Even after reaching the other shore, they continue to cling to the boat! Clinging blindly to the path instead of progressing along it, will only cause bondage.

If we want to reach the goal, it is our duty to follow the path prescribed by the scriptures, and to perform the required spiritual disciplines and practices. It is not enough to just study the scriptures. We also have to cultivate the attitude of bowing down to everything. The attitude of the ego prevails at present. We have to learn to bow down. When the grain grows into a rice plant, the plant automatically bends down. As it matures, the coconut bunch bows down from the palm tree. These examples teach us that when we develop perfect wisdom, we naturally become humble.

Studying the scriptures can be compared to building a wall around an orchard, while performing spiritual practice is like growing the fruit trees within those walls. The wall offers protection to the trees; but to get the actual fruits we have to plant the seedlings and cultivate them. This is absolutely necessary.

Studying the scriptures can also be compared to erecting a protective wall around our garden, while doing spiritual practice is like building a house within those walls, a house in which we are protected from the rain and the sun. Thus, studying the scriptures alone is not enough; observing the do's and don'ts on the spiritual path, meditating, repeating a mantra, and other spiritual practices are also necessary.

Once supreme love for God has awakened in the seeker, the various restrictions and observances are no longer essential. Before divine love, all restrictions and barriers dissolve. For a true devotee who possesses that love, there is only God. Throughout the whole universe, such a seeker sees only God. Just as the moth flies into the fire and merges with the flames, the devotee, in his or her love for God, becomes God in essence. The devotee, the universe itself—all is God. What rules and restrictions could apply to such a soul?

Through meditation, you can gain immense power. Just as all the water in a tank can flow through a single pipe, the Supreme Power flows through a tapasvi. The sage doesn't just sit there claiming to be Brahman. Because of the sage's compassion, the Power that flows through him or her benefits the whole world.

Question – Mother, why do you give so much importance to selfless service?

Mother – Meditation and studying the scriptures are like two sides of a coin. The engraving on that coin is selfless service, and that is what gives it its real value.

A student who has just completed his or her medical studies is still not competent enough to treat any patients. The student first has to work as an intern for a period of time. It is the experience gained during internship that gives the new doctor the necessary practical knowledge, and which allows him or her to apply what was studied. It is not enough if what you have studied remains nothing more than theoretical knowledge for your intellect: you have to translate it into action.

However much you study the scriptures, whatever level of spiritual learning you may have, you still have to train the mind to overcome trying situations; and the best way to do this is through karma yoga. It is when you go out into the world and work in various situations that you can see how your mind reacts to different circumstances. We cannot know ourselves unless we have been forced to face certain situations. When the right circumstances arise, your vasanas will raise their hoods. As we see the vasanas rise, one after the other, we can eliminate them. Selfless service strengthens the mind so that you can overcome any situation in life.

Our compassion and acts of selflessness take us to the deeper truths. Through selfless action we can eradicate the ego that conceals the Self. Detached, selfless action leads to liberation. Such action is not just work; it is karma yoga. Lord Krishna said to Arjuna, "In all the three worlds, there is nothing I need to do, nothing for me to attain, and yet I am ever engaged in action."

The Lord's actions were dispassionate and selfless. This is the path that Krishna advised Arjuna to follow.

A worshipper needs a smooth, round stone to use for a special religious ritual. Wandering in search of such a stone, the seeker finally climbs a mountain, hoping to find such a stone at the top. Finally reaching the mountaintop and discovering with a sense of great disappointment that there are no smooth, beautiful stones up there, the frustrated seeker grabs a rock and hurls it down the mountainside. After climbing back down and reaching the foot of the mountain, the seeker discovers a beautiful, smooth, perfectly shaped, round stone—just the type sought all along—

lying on the ground! Then he realizes that it is the same stone that was thrown down the mountain! On the way down it struck against other rough stones, and in this way it lost all its sharp edges. Had it remained on the mountaintop, it would never have been polished and transformed.

Similarly, when we move from the mountain top, that is, from the plane of the ego down to the plane of humility, the rough, sharp edges of our ego are removed, and the mind assumes an attitude of worship.

If we persist in cultivating the ego, nothing will be gained. By being humble, we gain everything.

A selfless, desireless attitude helps us to remove the ego. That is why unmotivated actions are given so much importance.

As long as the ego exists, the guidance of a spiritual master is needed. To a disciple who lives in accordance with the master's will, each action is a way to remove the sharp edges of the ego. There is no selfishness in the satguru. The master lives for the disciple. The disciple should take total refuge in the master. Just as a patient lies down without resisting and allows the doctor to operate on him or her, the disciple should surrender completely to the master's will.

Mother isn't saying that action alone is what leads us to the goal. Karma (action), jnana (knowledge), and bhakti (devotion) are all essential. If the two wings of a bird are devotion and action, knowledge is its tail. Only with the help of all three can the bird soar into the heights.

To be able to confront different situations in life with presence of mind and mental poise, we first have to train the mind. The field of action provides the ideal ground for this training. What the seeker does when his or her mind is intent on the goal is not just work; it is karma yoga—spiritual practice. For the spiritual aspirant, every action he or she performs is spiritual practice; as a disciple it is his or her way of serving the master (guru seva); as a devotee it is a form of worship. The master is not a person—the master is an embodiment of all divine qualities. The master is the Light. The master is like musk which at one moment has form and fragrance, and in the next evaporates. The master has a form—and yet, is formless. The master is beyond all forms and attributes. The master lives for the disciple, never for him- or herself. Every action the disciple performs with this understanding is karma yoga, leading to liberation. By serving a master in this way, the disciple attains the state of supreme consciousness.

Question – What is the most important requirement to progress in spiritual life?

Mother – When a flower is still a bud, we cannot experience its beauty or fragrance. The flower first has to blossom. It would be useless to try to open it by force. We have to wait patiently for the bud to unfold on its own. Only then can we fully experience its beauty and perfume. What is needed here is patience.

In every stone exists a latent image. When the sculptor chisels away all the unwanted parts, the image emerges. That beautiful form is born because the stone offers itself to the artist, sitting patiently before him or her for a long time.

A stone lying at the bottom of the Sabarimala mountain[26] complains to the image of the Lord that is wor-

26 A holy mountain in Kerala on top of which there is a sacred temple.

shipped in the temple, "You are a stone just like me, and yet you are worshipped by everyone, while I am being trampled. What justice is this?" The image replies: "Now you see only that everyone worships me. But before I came here, a sculptor chiseled away at me hundreds of thousands of times. During all that time, I lay patiently before the sculptor, without the slightest resistance. As a result of this, I am here now and am being worshipped by millions." The patience of the stone has transformed it into an image of worship.

Many people know the story of Kunti and Gandhari. It is a story that illustrates the benefit that comes from patience, and the harm that comes from impatience. When Kunti gave birth to a child, Gandhari, who was pregnant at the time, became upset. She badly longed for a child and had wanted her child to be born first, so that he would become king. In her extreme impatience, she beat her own stomach so hard that she miscarried and gave birth to a mass of flesh. Following the instructions of the sage Vyasa, the mass of flesh was cut into a hundred pieces and placed in a hundred urns. According to the story, in due course, a hundred sons were born out of the urns. This was the origin of the Kauravas, who were to cause the destruction of millions of people. Gandhari didn't have any patience, and this resulted in so much suffering and destruction. On the other hand, what is born out of patience becomes victorious. In spiritual life, patience is vitally important.

We should always have the attitude of being a beginner, the attitude of an innocent child. Only a beginner has the patience and attentiveness required to really learn. There is a child in each of us. At present it is slumbering, that is all. We have to awaken that child. The sense of "I" that exists now is a creation of the ego. When the sleeping child within us is awakened, our innocent nature will emerge naturally. We will feel a desire to learn from everything. Patience, awareness and attentiveness will follow of their own accord. Thus, when the inner child awakens, those qualities will blossom within us. The old "I", the "I" that was created by the ego, will no longer have a place. If we always have the attitude of a beginner, every situation will be an opportunity for us to learn. Whatever we need will come to us. If we can maintain this attitude throughout life until the very end, we won't lose anything. We will gain everything.

Today most people know only the laughter displayed by the teeth. True laughter comes from the heart. Only with an innocent heart can we experience real joy and give joy to others. For this we have to awaken the heart of the innocent child within us. We have to nurture that child. The saying, "If you become a zero, you will become a hero," is about the disappearance of the "I" born from the ego.

Question – Mother, you seem to be giving more importance to bhakti (devotion) than to any other path. Why is this so?

Mother – Children, when you say "devotion," do you mean just repeating a mantra and singing devotional songs? Real devotion is to discriminate between the eternal and the transitory; it is to surrender yourself to the Infinite. What Mother advises is the practical side of devotion.

The children who live here read many books and they

ask Mother questions. Mother usually gives them answers along the lines of Vedanta. But when talking to people in general, Mother gives more importance to devotion, because ninety percent of the people are not intellectual. They haven't learned any spiritual science before coming here. It isn't possible to teach them the spiritual principles in just one day or during one darshan. It is therefore wiser to give them advice that they can actually live by. Mother also advises them to read spiritual books.

Advaita (non-duality) is the foundation of everything. What Mother teaches is practical devotion that is rooted in advaita.

Most of the people who come here are ignorant about spiritual matters. They are familiar only with going to temples. Only about ten percent of them may give some importance to knowledge and reason and may follow a different path. But we cannot neglect the others. Don't they also need to be uplifted? So Mother gives advice according to the level of each person.

The prayers and devotional singing at the ashram are not just prayers—they are spiritual practices done to awaken the real "I" (Self) within us. It is a process of tuning the individual consciousness to the Universal Consciousness, of tuning into the Universal Self from the level of body, mind, and intellect.

There is no need to search for a God sitting somewhere beyond the sky. God is the all-pervading Universal Consciousness. Still, we advise people to meditate on a form, because a medium is necessary to make the mind one-pointed. To construct a slab of concrete, we first have to make a wooden frame, and it is into that frame that we pour the concrete. When the concrete has set, we can remove the frame. This can be compared to worshipping a divine form. The form is required in the beginning until the principles are firmly grasped. Once the mind is firmly established in the Universal Self, there is no longer any need for any such tools.

Only those who are humble can receive God's grace. In someone who perceives God's presence in everything, there is no room for the ego. So, the first quality we need to develop within ourselves is humility. That is the purpose of the prayers and devotional singing in the ashram. We should be humble in our every look, word, and deed.

When a carpenter picks up a chisel to begin his work, he touches it reverentially and bows to it to invoke a blessing. The chisel is just an instrument he uses for his work, and yet he bows to it. We pick up the harmonium only after touching it with reverence and bowing to it. It is part of our culture to show reverence toward something before using it. But why do we show such respect to the objects we use? It is to behold God in everything that we do this. What our ancestors were aiming at through this practice was a state of egolessness. Similarly, prayer is an expression of humility; it is a way to eliminate the ego.

Some people may ask if prayers can't be done in silence. For some people it may be necessary to read in silence, while for others reading aloud is more effective. Some people can understand things only if they read aloud. We cannot tell someone who reads aloud when studying, "Don't read so loudly! You should read quietly, like me!" Some people get more concentration by praying aloud, while others prefer to pray quietly. Similarly, for different types of people different spiritual paths are required. All paths lead to the ultimate stillness.

Many people say, "Mother, when I meditate with my eyes closed, a lot of thoughts continuously arise in the mind, but when I sing bhajans (devotional songs) and pray, I get full concentration." The purpose of spiritual practice is to make the mind one-pointed. When we say, "I am not the body, nor the mind, nor the intellect," thus following the "neti, neti" ("not this, not this") path, we are using another way to reach the Supreme Being. The purpose of prayers and bhajans is the same.

Is there any religion in which devotion and prayer do not have a place? You will find both devotion and prayer in Buddhism, Christianity, and Islam. All these religions also have the master-disciple relationship. The master-disciple relationship can even be found on the non-dualistic path. So even on that path, in the master-disciple relationship, duality exists. Isn't devotion to the master devotion itself?

Through our prayers we are trying to imbibe divine qualities; we are trying to realize the Absolute. Prayer is not a way of weakness—it is a powerful step toward God.

Question – Can meditation be harmful? Some people say that their heads feel hot during meditation.

Mother – It is always best to learn how to meditate directly from a master. Meditation is like a health tonic. A tonic comes with certain instructions. If you ignore the instructions and swallow all the contents at once, it could be harmful. Similarly, you should meditate according to the directions of a spiritual master. The master first makes an assessment of your mental and physical disposition before prescribing the form of spiritual practice that is most suitable for you. Some people can meditate for any length of time without any problem. But that is not the case with everyone. Some people meditate for a long time continuously in a sudden surge of enthusiasm, without following any rules or regulations. They don't even bother to sleep. Their practice isn't based on any understanding of the spiritual texts or on the instructions of an adept. They just do it in a burst of enthusiasm. They won't be able to get enough sleep, and their heads will become hot. This happens because they are meditating more than the body can tolerate. Everyone has a certain capacity, depending on the state of his or her own mind and body. If five hundred people are crammed into a vehicle which can seat only a hundred, the vehicle won't be able to move properly. If you put twice as much grain as suggested into a small grinder, the motor will get overheated; it may even burn up. Similarly, if, in a surge of initial enthusiasm, you do japa and meditation indiscriminately for long hours, your head may become hot and many other problems may occur. This is why it is advised that one should do these practices under the guidance of a satguru.

There are people who say, "Everything is within me. I myself am God." But those are just words. It doesn't come from experience. The capacity of each instrument is limited. A ten-watt bulb cannot give the light of a hundred-watt bulb. A generator provides power, but if it is given a larger load than it can sustain, it will burn out. There is a limit to the amount of spiritual practice one can do. It depends on the capacity of the mind and body. You have to be careful so that you don't exceed the limit.

If you buy a brand-new car, you shouldn't drive it too fast in the beginning. To make it last long and function smoothly, it should be handled gently. It is the same with the seeker in his or her spiritual practice. Japa and meditation should not be done in excess and to the total exclusion of sleep. Meditation, japa, scriptural studies, and physical work should be done in a regulated way. There are people who are prone to mental imbalance or delusions. If they meditate too much, their bodies get overheated and this aggravates their mental condition. They should engage mainly in physical work. This will help reduce their mental imbalance. When such people are engaged in work, their minds will wander less and can gradually be controlled. If they are allowed to just sit, without doing any physical work, their condition will only worsen. They can meditate for ten to fifteen minutes a day if they are not under any tension; that is enough for them.

Thus, there are many different types of people. Each individual has to be given different instructions. If you learn how to do spiritual practices, such as meditation, just by reading books, you will not know what restrictions are required specifically for you, and this could cause problems.

Suppose you are about to visit a house where there is an aggressive dog outside. You will call the owner from outside the gate, and wait until she has come and tied up the dog, so that it cannot harm you. Only then do you step inside. If you don't have any patience and just open the gate and try to enter, the dog is likely to bite you. Similarly, it could be dangerous if you just go ahead with your spiritual practice, without accepting the advice of a wise, experienced person.

The seeker is on a journey through a forest full of dangers, including ferocious wild animals. The traveler needs the help of a guide who knows the way through the forest. Isn't it best to have someone with us who can tell us: "There's danger just ahead. Be careful! Don't go that way! Go that way instead!"?

It is useless to blame God when we suffer the consequences of ignoring the wise guidelines we have been given, and just do as we like. When we blame God for the consequences of our own lack of attention, we are a bit like the drunkard who went for a drive. The car went out of control and hit another car. When the police arrested drunk driver, he protested and said, "Sir, it wasn't my fault that my car hit that car! Surely, the petrol is to blame!" We are doing much the same thing if we blame God for the dangers we face owing to our own lack of caution.

Everything has its own dharma—its own codes, rules, and inherent nature—and we should live in accordance with that dharma. Meditation, too, has its own methodology. The masters have laid down the rules and methods for each type of spiritual practice. An appropriate method of spiritual practice should be adopted after taking into account the seeker's physical and mental disposition. The same method isn't suitable for everyone.

Anyone can learn theories by reading a book. But to be successful in practical tests, you need the assistance of a learned instructor, because it is difficult to master the practical aspects of a subject on your own. In the same way, the seeker needs a competent master who can guide him or her on the spiritual path.

Question – If non-duality is the ultimate truth, what is the need of Devi Bhava?

Mother – Mother is not confined to any bhava (divine mood or attitude). She is beyond all bhavas. Isn't advaita an experience? Where there are not two, everything is the essence of the Self alone—everything is God. This is the message Mother is giving through Her Devi Bhava. To Mother, there are no distinctions. She knows all as the one Self. Mother has come for the sake of the world. Her life is for the sake of the world.

Whatever role an actor plays, he knows who he really is. It makes no difference to the actor what role he plays. Likewise, whatever role Mother plays, She knows Herself, and is not bound by anything. She didn't take on this role by Herself. She gave in to the devotees' wishes. They then surrendered to this Bhava. They rejoice in it.

Mother goes to many places in North India. There, Krishna devotees often come to see Her. They place a crown with peacock feathers on Mother's head, they put a flute in Mother's hands, they dress Her in yellow silk, give Her butter, and do arati. They delight in this, and Mother accepts it because it makes them happy. Mother would never say to them, "I am a Vedantin, so I can't accept this!"

God is formless and attributeless. At the same time, He has forms and attributes. God is the Consciousness that is everywhere and in everything. Because of this we can behold God in any Bhava.

Mother did not don any special costume in the early days. The devotees brought these clothes and items, one by one. It was for their happiness and contentment that Mother started wearing them, and thus it became a ritual.

In a temple, there is always an image of a deity, but people accord the deity greater importance during the daily deepa-aradhana.[27] At that time, the image is dressed in a special costume and ornaments. This gives the devotees greater joy and concentration. Many people go to temples every day, but during the temple festival days the crowds are much larger. The whole village will celebrate. Similarly, even though people come here to see Mother every day, the Devi Bhava is like a special festival for them.

Temple worship is not done for God's sake, but for the happiness and satisfaction of the devotees. Similarly, Mother wears all these costumes for the sake of Her children, and by doing so, Mother is removing their "costumes." Mother is gradually elevating them to the experience of their real nature.

Today everyone in the world lives in costume. People have different hairstyles, apply marks on their foreheads, and dress in different fashions. We cannot separate costume from life because it is an integral part of life. Each type of dress has its own relevance. The costumes of a monk, a lawyer, and a policeman create different reactions in us.

A man was illegally cutting timber in a forest. A plain-clothed policeman approached him and tried to prevent him from doing so, but the man ignored him. The policeman left and returned wearing his uniform. Seeing the uniformed policeman even from a distance, the man took to his heels. Such is the significance of a costume.

A big party was being held. All the guests were dressed in expensive clothes and jewelry. Then one of the guests

27 Literally, "lamp worship." Offering a lamp and then burning camphor to the Deity by waving them before the image in circles.

arrived wearing ordinary clothes. The doorman refused to let him in. The man went home and returned wearing a formal suit. This time he was allowed to enter. When he reached the dining table he removed his jacket and placed it in front of a dish. He took off his hat and put it next to a plate, and placed his tie in front of a teacup. The other guests thought he was crazy. He turned to them and said, "When I arrived here in my ordinary clothes, they wouldn't let me in. When I came in this suit, I was immediately allowed to enter. From this I gather that it wasn't I, but my clothes that were invited to this party."

This is what the world is like today. People place their faith in external appearances. They try to attract others with their costumes. Rare are those who look for the inner beauty. The purpose of Mother's costume is to remove all forms of costumes; it is to help people to realize their true nature. When a thorn is stuck in your foot, you remove it with another thorn.

The Vedantins who talk about advaita do not walk around without any clothes. They wear clothes and eat and sleep like everyone else. They know that all this is necessary for the existence of the body, and they dress in accordance with the customs of the society in which they live.

The mahatmas are born according to the need of the times. Sri Rama and Sri Krishna came in different ages. Whatever they did was in answer to the need of the time in which they lived. It is meaningless to say that Krishna has to be exactly like Rama. Each divine incarnation is unique.

A doctor usually has many patients. He doesn't prescribe the same medicine to everyone. Only after assessing the illness and the nature of a patient is he able to determine what sort of treatment is necessary for that individual. For some, oral medication is enough, while others need to be given injections. In a similar way, on the spiritual path, the need of each individual varies. We have to go down to the level of each person who comes here in order to uplift him or her.

The same kind of candies are wrapped in different-colored wrappers. Outwardly they appear to be different, but inside they are the same. Similarly, it is the same Consciousness that dwells in everything. It isn't possible to teach this principle to people without first coming down to their level. But instead of just staying at that level with them, our aim is to bring them to the awareness of that oneness. This is what Mother is doing.

You cannot talk about advaita to everyone. Not everyone can understand the concept of the Formless and Attributeless. There are a few rare individuals who can progress along the path of advaita after it has been explained to them. They have been born with the mental disposition required for this. But most people cannot comprehend advaita in its depth.

Some people like Radha-Krishna (Krishna as the Beloved of the gopi Radha) the most; others prefer Yashoda-Krishna (Krishna as the child of Yashoda); while still others adore Murali-Krishna (the flute-playing Krishna). All people have their own preferences that give them joy. People also experience Mother in different ways. Mother doesn't say that everyone has to find joy in one particular aspect.

Mother assumes certain bhavas in order to come down to the level of the people, to make them aware of the underlying oneness which is beyond all bhavas. Mother has to act according to the nature of the people. Her aim is to lead people to the Truth by any means. That which helps to uplift people—that alone is truly rational. Mother is concerned only with uplifting people. This is all She wants. Mother doesn't need any certificate of approval from the world.

A person stands on a balcony looking down, and sees someone below, lying helpless in the dirt. She cannot save that person by stretching out her hand from where she stands. She has to go down, take hold of his hands and lift him up. Similarly, in order to uplift people spiritually we have to come down to their level.

To reach the main road, we have to go through certain side streets. Once we get there, there will be no lack of express buses and we can proceed straight to our destination. But we still have to get to the main road in some way, and for that we may need a bicycle or a rickshaw. Similarly, we have to adopt different means to lead people along the narrow roads of bondage, in order to help them reach the main road of Vedanta.

Question – Mother, is it true that we can enjoy spiritual bliss only if we see this world as unreal and renounce it?

Mother – Mother doesn't say we should dismiss this world as totally unreal. The meaning of the word "unreal" here is that something is constantly changing. If we depend on such things, if we become attached to them, we will experience only sorrow. This is what Mother means. The body also changes. Don't feel too attached to the body. Every cell of the body is changing every instant. Life itself goes through different stages—infancy, childhood, youth, middle age and old age. Don't look upon the body as real and devote your entire life to it. As you proceed through life, try to understand the nature of everything. Then you won't have to suffer. Imagine that you have a valuable diamond. You could make a beautiful piece of jewelry from it. If you instead were to eat it you could die. Likewise, there is an intended use for everything in life. If we can understand this, there won't be any reason for us to suffer. This is why it is advised that people learn about spirituality. Isn't it better to learn how to avoid a fall before we might fall, than to look for a solution after we have already fallen? An understanding of the spiritual principles is the most important type of knowledge we can have in life.

A dog chews on a bone. It enjoys the taste of blood and continues to chew. Only in the end, when its gums start hurting, does the dog realize it has been tasting its own blood coming from its lacerated gums. This is what our search for happiness in external things is like. It causes us to lose all our strength. In truth, happiness does not lie in external objects, but is to be found within ourselves. We should lead our lives with an understanding of this principle.

Question – The vast majority of people today are interested in worldly matters only. Hardly anyone is interested in looking inward. What message does Mother have for society?

Mother – Our lives shouldn't be like that of a dog that barks at its own reflection in a mirror, taking it to be real. We shouldn't chase after shadows, but should turn inward. Mother has one message to impart—it is a message based on having met several million people who are living both spiritual and worldly lives—and that is that you will not experience peace in this life as long as you don't give up your excessive fascination with the external world.

Question – Is it possible to enjoy spiritual bliss while still living in this world?

Mother – Certainly. That bliss is to be experienced while you are still in this world—in the body. It isn't something to be attained after death.

Like the mind and body, spirituality and worldliness are two facets of life. They cannot exist totally separated from each other. Spirituality is the science that teaches us how to live happily in the material world.

There are two types of education. One type of education will enable you to find a suitable job; the other shows you how to live a life of peace and happiness. That is spirituality. It is the knowledge of the mind.

When you are traveling to a new place, there won't be anything to worry about if you have a reliable map. Similarly, if you use the principles of spirituality as a guide and live your life accordingly, you will never be overwhelmed by any crises. You will know how to foresee and deal with any situation. Spirituality is the practical science of life. It teaches us the nature of the world, how to understand life and live fully in the best way possible.

We enter the water so that we can come out fresh and

clean. We don't intend to remain in the water forever. Similarly, living a householder's life is a way of removing the obstacles on the path to God. Once we have adopted the life of a householder, we should be aware of the real purpose of life and move forward. Our life shouldn't end where we began. We are meant to free ourselves from all bonds and to realize God.

The attitude of "mine" is the cause of all bondage. Family life should be seen as an opportunity to liberate us from that attitude. You say, "my wife or husband, my children, my parents," etc. But are they really yours? If they really belonged to you they would be with you forever. Only when we live with this awareness can we really awaken spirituality. This doesn't mean we should abandon our responsibilities. We should joyfully do whatever needs to be done in life, seeing it as our duty. But we should be careful so that we don't become attached to it.

There is a difference between the attitude of a person who is appearing for a job interview and someone who is about to start a job she has already secured. The person who is about to be interviewed will be worried about what sort of questions will be asked, whether he will be able to answer them properly, and whether he will finally get the job. The applicant's mind will be tense. For the other person who is reporting for work, it is quite different because she has already been chosen for the job and will feel a certain happiness. We will also experience a certain joy in our lives once we understand the principles of spirituality; because then, like the person who has found a job, we no longer have any reason to worry.

Suppose you need some money and are thinking about

asking a friend for help. You know that she may give you the money, but, then, on the other hand, chances are she won't. If she feels generous and decides to help you, you could get more than you expected; but she could also turn her back on you and even pretend she doesn't know you. If you are aware of all these possibilities beforehand, you won't feel surprised or disappointed, whatever the outcome.

An expert swimmer greatly enjoys swimming among the waves of the sea, whereas a person who hasn't learned how to swim would drown among those same waves. Similarly, those who understand the principles of spirituality enjoy every moment of life. They face every situation with a smile; nothing can unsettle them. Look at the life of Lord Krishna. Even when His family and clansmen, the Yadavas, were fighting amongst themselves, the smile on His lips never faded. That smile didn't fade even when He held discussions with the Kauravas as an envoy for the Pandavas. When He acted as Arjuna's charioteer on the battlefield, a wonderful smile lit His lips. He bore that same smile when Gandhari cursed him. Krishna's whole life was a big smile. If we allow spirituality into our lives, we will experience real joy.

Life should be like a pleasure trip. When we see a beautiful sight, a pretty house, or a flower on the way, we look at it and enjoy it. We enjoy the sights but we do not linger there; we simply move on. When it's time to return, no matter how beautiful the things around us are, we leave them behind and go home, because there is nothing more important to us than getting back home. Similarly, in whatever manner we live in this world, we shouldn't forget our real home to which we must return—we should never forget our goal. No matter how many beautiful sights we may see on our way through life, there is only one place that we can call our own, where we can rest, and that is our point of origin—the Self.

A father had four children. As he grew old, his adult sons and daughters pressed him to divide his property and give them each a plot. They wanted to build separate houses on that land. "We will look after you. There are four of us, so you can stay with each of us for three months during the year. You will be happy that way." The father was happy when all four of them suggested this. And so the property was divided. The family house and the adjoining plot were given to the eldest son, and the other three were given their shares of the land on which they each built a house. After the division, the father went to stay with the eldest son. For the first few days he was treated with much warmth and respect. But the family's enthusiasm in looking after the old man soon diminished. As the days went by, the faces of his son and daughter-in-law darkened. It was difficult for the father, but somehow he forced himself to stay for a month until he felt they were about to turn him out. He then left and went to stay with his second eldest, a daughter. This daughter and her husband also showed some enthusiasm in the beginning, but they soon changed, and he was forced to leave after only fifteen days. He then went to his third child's home, but ended up staying there for only ten days because they really didn't want him there. And so he went to stay with his youngest child. After only five days he discovered that they were about to throw him out. And so he left and spent the rest of his life wandering about without a place to live.

When the father divided his property among his four children, he hoped that they would take care of him in his final days. But that was just a dream. After barely two months, he had been abandoned by his whole family.

We should understand that this is what human love is often like. If we have the expectation that certain people will eventually look after us, it will only lead to sorrow. So, we should cheerfully carry out our duties, without any expectations, and when the time is right we should turn to our true path, the spiritual path.

This doesn't mean what we have to give up our responsibilities. We should fulfill our dharma. It is, for example, the duty of parents to take care of their children; but once the children have grown up and can take care of themselves, the parents shouldn't continue to be attached to them and expect their children to look after them. We should be aware of the real goal of life and continue our journey toward that. We shouldn't limit ourselves by focusing only on our children and grandchildren.

The bird perching on a dry twig is always alert, ready to fly up, because it knows that the twig could break at any moment. Likewise, as we live in this world, performing various actions, we should always be watchful, ready to soar into the world of the Self, knowing that nothing in this world is eternal. Then, nothing can bind us or make us sorrowful.

Question – Mother, you often say that if we take one step toward God, God will take a hundred steps toward us. Does this mean that God is far away from us?

Mother – No. It means that if you make an effort to

cultivate just one good quality, all the other good qualities will develop naturally within you.

A woman was once given a beautiful crystal chandelier as first prize in an art competition. She hung it in her drawing room. While enjoying its beauty, she observed that some of the paint on the wall had begun to crumble. She decided to paint the whole wall. When she had finished painting, she looked at the room and noticed that a window curtain was dirty. She immediately washed all the curtains. Then it came to her attention that the old rug on the floor had become threadbare. So she removed the carpet and replaced it with a new one. Finally, the room looked like new. It all began with her hanging the new lamp in the room, and ended up with the room becoming clean and beautiful, having undergone a complete transformation. Similarly, if you begin to do one good thing in life regularly, many good things will follow naturally in its wake—it will be like a rebirth. God is the source of all good qualities. If we imbibe any one of them, all other virtues will follow. This is the only way in which a transformation is possible.

Students are often awarded grace marks to help them pass their examinations. Though everyone is eligible, only those who have secured a minimum level can receive them. So it calls for effort on the part of the students. Similarly, God is constantly showering His grace upon us. But if we are to benefit from that grace, there has to be some effort on our part as well. If our minds don't have the receptivity needed, then even if God pours His grace upon us, it won't do us any good. What is the use of complaining about the lack of sunlight, when we ourselves have closed all the doors and window shutters of our room? The sun shines its light everywhere. We need only open the doors and windows to experience it. Similarly, God is constantly bestowing His grace upon us, but we have to open the doors of our hearts to receive that grace. This means that before we can receive God's grace, we first have to receive the grace of our own mind. God is infinitely compassionate. It is our own mind that lacks compassion toward us, and acts as an obstacle, hindering us from receiving God's grace.

If someone extends a hand toward us with a gift, and we are arrogant toward that person, he or she will withdraw the hand, thinking, "What a big ego! I don't think I'll give my gift to that person after all. I'd rather give it to someone else." Thus we have failed to give ourselves the grace needed to receive that gift. This was caused by our ego. We could not receive what was being offered to us because our own mind didn't have any compassion toward us.

On certain occasions, our discriminating intellect tells us to do something. But our mind refuses to agree. The intellect says, "Be humble," while the mind says, "No! I'm not going to be humble before these people!" The result is that much of what we could have gained is lost to us. What we could have achieved remains out of our reach.

To receive God's grace we first need the grace of our own Self. This is why Mother always says, "My children, always have the attitude of a beginner!" Having that attitude will prevent the hood of the ego from rising.

You may ask, "If I always remain a beginner, won't that mean that I'll never make any progress?" Not at all. Having the attitude of a beginner means that you retain the total openness, attentiveness, and receptivity of a beginner. This is the only way to truly imbibe wisdom and knowledge.

You may wonder how you can function in society and do your work if you're always innocent and childlike. But to be innocent and childlike doesn't mean to be a weakling—far from it! You have to be strong and assertive if the situations so demand. But, still, you should always, as far as possible, be as open and receptive as a child.

Everything has its own dharma, and we have to act according to that. If a cow chews up a precious plant, and we politely tell it to move, saying, "My dear cow, would you mind moving?" of course it's not going to move. On the other hand, if we shout "Hey cow! Move!" then the cow will go away. We cannot call this action egoistic; it is a role we adopt to correct the ignorance of another being, and there's nothing wrong with this. But we should always have a profound inner attitude of being a beginner, retaining the innocence of a child.

Nowadays, peoples' bodies have grown, but their minds are not expansive. To make the mind expand and embrace the whole universe, you should first become a child. Only a child can grow. But the minds of today are full of egotism. Our effort should be directed toward destroying the ego within us. That means being perfectly tuned to others. Say that two cars are heading toward each other on a narrow road. If both drivers refuse to yield and give way, neither of them can move forward. But if just one of them is prepared to back up a little, they can both proceed.

Here, the one who compromises and yields and the one who receives that gesture are both able to go forward.

This is why it is said that to yield is to go forward. It will uplift both the person who yields and the one who receives the courtesy. We should always look at the practical side. The ego is always a hindrance to progress.

God is always compassionate toward us. He bestows His grace upon us constantly, more so than we deserve by our actions. God is not just a judge who rewards us for our good deeds and punishes us for our sins—God is compassion itself, the Fountain of infinite grace. He forgives our mistakes and showers His grace upon us. But God can save us only if there is at least a little effort on our part. If we make no effort at all, we cannot receive the grace that is being offered to us by God, who is the Ocean of Compassion. So we can't consider anything to be God's fault—it is our fault.

When Princess Rukmini was about to be given away in marriage, it was because she held her arms out toward Lord Krishna that He could lift her into His chariot and whisk her away.[28] Thus there has to be a positive reaching out or effort on our part.

During a job interview, some candidates may not answer every question properly but are nevertheless selected. The compassion of the interviewer is responsible for this. That is divine grace. On the other hand, many candidates are not selected even if they answer all the questions perfectly, and have all the needed qualifications and numerous references. The divine grace that worked through the

---

28 Princess Rukmini of Vidarbha loved Krishna and wanted Him to be her husband. She sent a messenger to Krishna requesting Him to claim her on the day she was supposed to be given in marriage to King Sisupala. Krishna came to the ceremony and whisked her away in His chariot, fighting off everyone who tried to stop Him.

interviewer was not available to them. This shows us that when we make an effort, divine grace is also needed. This grace depends on our previous actions. Our ego stops us from receiving grace.

We are not isolated islands. Our lives are interconnected like the links of a chain. We are part of the chain of life. Whether we are aware of it or not, our every action has an effect on others.

It isn't right to think that we will become good only when everyone else has changed. We should be willing to change even if no one else does so. Thinking that we will change for the better only after those around us have changed is like hoping to enter the sea after all the waves have subsided. Instead of waiting for others to improve, we should make an effort to improve ourselves. Then we will begin to see changes in others as well. When we cultivate only goodness in ourselves, we will see only goodness in others. So we should be careful about our every thought and deed.

Our lives should be filled with compassion. We should be ready to help the poor. No one is above fault. Whenever we see a fault in anyone, we should immediately look within ourselves. Then we will recognize that the fault is to be found within ourselves.

Even if someone gets angry, we should understand it is his or her samskara (the totality of impressions and deep-rooted tendencies acquired during countless lives). Then we will be able to forgive the angry person; we will have the strength to forgive. Our attitude of forgiveness will make our thoughts, words, and actions good. Our good deeds will draw God's grace to us. Just as good actions bring good fruits, negative actions can bring only negative results. Negative actions are the cause of suffering. So we should always take care that our actions are good; then divine grace will flow to us. Once we have received this grace, we will have no reason to complain that life is sorrowful.

Life is like the pendulum of a clock, constantly moving back and forth in opposite directions, from sorrow to happiness and back again. To be able to accept both joy and sorrow, and to progress spiritually, we need to have an understanding of spirituality. In this way we can easily overcome the momentum that builds up in either direction. We will understand the true nature of everything. Meditation is the method we use for this.

Even in a person who is evil there is an inherent possibility of becoming good. There is no human being who doesn't posses at least one divine quality. With patience we can awaken the divinity in a person. We should try to cultivate this attitude. When we perceive the goodness in everything, we will be filled with God's grace. That grace is the source of all success in life.

If we all turn our backs on a person, thinking only of the wrongs he or she has committed, what future does that person have? On the other hand, if we perceive the little good that is still there and encourage that person to cultivate that quality, he or she will be uplifted. This could have such an effect that he or she may even become a great person. Sri Rama was willing to prostrate before Queen Kaikeyi, who was responsible for His banishment to the forest. Christ washed Judas's feet, even though He knew that Judas was about to betray him. When the woman who had once thrown dirt on the Prophet Mohammed fell ill, He came to her and nursed her without being asked to do so. Such are the examples shown to us by the great souls. The easiest way to experience constant peace and happiness in life is to follow the path they have shown us.

Divinity lies dormant in everyone. By trying to awaken the divinity in others, we are, in fact, awakening the divinity within ourselves.

There was once a master who wished to move to a certain village. He sent two of his disciples to that village to investigate what the people were like who lived there. One of the disciples visited the place and soon returned. He said to the master, "All the people in that village are the most wicked people imaginable! They are robbers, killers, and prostitutes! Nowhere else will you find such evil souls."

When the second disciple returned, he said to the master, "The people in that village are very good. Never before have I met such good people." The master wondered how the two disciples could have such contrasting opinions about the same village. When he asked them to explain, the first disciple said, "In the first house I entered, I was greeted by a murderer; in the second house lived a robber, and in the third house I saw a prostitute. I felt so discouraged that I didn't bother to go any further. I quickly left the place and came back here. How can I say anything good about a village where such bad people reside?"

The master turned to the second disciple and asked him to describe what he had seen. The disciple said, "I went to the same houses as he did. At the first house I met a robber. When I came there he was busy feeding the poor. He is in the habit of finding the starving people in the village and feeding them. When I saw this good quality in him, I was overjoyed.

"In the second house I visited lived a murderer. When I got there, he was outside taking care of a poor man who was lying on the road. It struck me that even though he was a murderer, he still had some compassion; his heart was not entirely dry. When I saw this, I felt so much love for him. I then went to the third house, which belonged to a prostitute. There were four children in the house. When I asked about them, I was told they were orphans whom the prostitute had taken under her wing and was raising. So when I discovered that there were such wonderful qualities in those who are considered to be the worst people in the village, I couldn't even imagine how much more noble the other villagers must be! Thus, by visiting those three houses, I was given a great impression of the people of that village."

To turn one's back on people, claiming that there is only evil everywhere—that is the way of the lazy. If, instead of talking about the evil of others, we were to do all we could to awaken the goodness within ourselves, then we could give light to others. This is the easiest way to change ourselves—and society as well—for the better. Instead of blaming the encircling darkness, light your own little candle. Don't feel daunted at the thought of trying to dispel the darkness of the world with the small light within you. If you simply light your candle and move forward, it will shine its light at every step of your way, and will benefit those around you.

So, my children, let us light the wick of love within us and move forward. When we take each step forward with positive thoughts and a smile, all good qualities will come to us and fill our being. Then God cannot possibly stay away from us. He will take us in His arms and hold us. Every moment of our lives will be filled with harmony and peace.

Glossary

Advaita – Non-dualism. The philosophy which teaches that the Supreme Reality is "One without a second."

Ahimsa – Nonviolence. Refraining from hurting any living being by thought, word, or deed.

Arati – The ritual in which light is offered in the form of burning camphor, and a bell is rung before the Deity in a temple or before a holy person, as a consummation of puja (worship). The camphor does not leave behind any residue; this symbolizes the total annihilation of the ego.

Ardhanarisvara – A half-male and half-female deity, symbolizing the Divinity that is the union of Shiva and Shakti, God and Goddess.

Arjuna – The third of the five Pandava brothers. A great archer who is one of the heroes of the Mahabharata. He was Krishna's friend and disciple. It is Arjuna whom Krishna is addressing in the Bhagavad Gita.

Ashram – "Place of striving." A place where spiritual seekers and aspirants live or visit in order to lead a spiritual life and perform spiritual practices. It is usually the home of a spiritual master, saint or ascetic, who guides the aspirants.

Asura – Demon.

Atman – The true Self. The essential nature of our real existence. One of the fundamental tenets of Sanatana Dharma is that we are not the physical body, feelings, mind, intellect or personality. We are the eternal, pure, unblemishable Self.

Bhagavad Gita – "Song of the Blessed One." Bhagavad = of the Lord; gita = song, referring particularly to advice. The teachings Lord Krishna gave Arjuna on the Kurukshetra battlefield at the beginning of the Mahabharata War. It is a practical guide for daily life and contains the essence of Vedic wisdom.

Bhajan – Devotional song.

Bhakti – Devotion and love.

Bhava – Divine mood or attitude.

Bhava darshan – The occasion when Mother receives devotees in the bhava of the Divine Mother.

Bhishma – The grandfather of the Pandavas and the Kauravas. Though he fought on the side of the Kauravas during the Mahabharata War, he was a champion of dharma and was sympathetic to the Pandavas. After Lord Krishna he is the most important character in the Mahabharata.

Brahma – The aspect of God associated with creation.

Brahmachari – A celibate disciple, who practices spiritual disciplines and is usually being trained by a spiritual master.

Brahmacharya – "Moving in Brahman." Celibacy and discipline of the mind and the senses.

Brahman – The Absolute Reality, Supreme Being; the Whole; that which encompasses and pervades everything, and is One and indivisible.

Darshan – An audience with or a vision of the Divine or of a holy person.

Deva – Celestial being.

Devi Bhava – "The Divine Mood of Devi." The state in which Mother reveals Her oneness and identity with the Divine Mother.

Dharma – In Sanskrit dharma means "that which upholds (Creation)." Most commonly it is used to indicate that which is responsible for the harmony of the universe. Dharma has many meanings, including the divine law, the law of existence, righteousness, religion, duty, responsibility, virtue, justice, goodness and truth. Dharma signifies the inner principles of religion. One well-known definition of dharma is that it leads to the spiritual uplift and general well-being of all beings in Creation. The opposite of dharma is adharma.

Gopi – The gopis were cowherd girls and milk maids who lived in Vrindavan. They were Krishna's closest devotees and were known for their supreme devotion to the Lord. They exemplify the most intense love for God.

Grihasthashrama – A spiritually orientated family life. This is traditionally the second stage of life. The stages are: brahmacharya (the period of education), grihasthashrama (living as a householder), vanaprastha (renouncing worldly responsibilities and dedicating one's life fully to spiritual practice), and sannyasa (renouncing all worldly attachments).

Grihasthashrami – Someone who is dedicated to leading a spiritual life, while at the same time carrying out his or her responsibilities as a householder.

Guna: Primal Nature (prakriti) consists of three gunas, i.e., fundamental qualities, tendencies or stresses, which underlie all manifestation: sattva (goodness, purity, serenity), rajas (activity, passion) and tamas (darkness, inertia, ignorance). These three gunas continually act and react with each other. The phenomenal world is composed of different combinations of the three gunas.

Guru – "One who removes the darkness of ignorance." Spiritual master/guide.

Gurukula – A gurukula is traditionally an ashram with a living spiritual master, where students and disciples live, studying with the master.

Japa – Repetition of a mantra, a prayer, or one of God's Names.

Jivatman – The individual soul.

Jnana – Spiritual knowledge and wisdom. Knowledge of the true nature of the world and its underlying reality. It is a direct experience, beyond any possible perception of the limited mind, intellect, or senses. It is attained through spiritual practice and the grace of God or the guru.

Kali – "The Dark One." The destroyer of kala (time). An aspect of the Divine Mother. From the viewpoint of the ego, She may seem frightening because She destroys the ego. But She destroys the ego and transforms us only out of Her immeasurable compassion. A devotee knows that behind Her fierce facade, the loving Mother is to be found, who protects Her children and bestows the grace of Liberation.

Karma – Action, deed

Karma yoga – "Union through action." The spiritual path of detached, selfless service and of dedicating the action and its fruits to God.

Kauravas – The one hundred children of Dhritharasthra and Gandhari, of whom Duryodhana was the eldest. The Kauravas were the enemies of their cousins, the Pandavas, whom they fought in the Mahabharata War.

Kshatriya – The warrior caste

Mahabharata – One of the two great Indian historic epics (Itihasa), the other being the *Ramayana*. It is a great treatise on dharma and spirituality. The story deals mainly with the conflict between the Pandavas and Kauravas, and the great war at Kurukshetra. The Mahabharata, which is the longest epic poem in the world, was written about 3200 B.C by the Sage Vyasa.

Mahatma – Great soul

Mantra – Sacred formula or prayer which is constantly repeated. This awakens one's dormant spiritual powers and helps one to reach the goal. It is most effective if received from a spiritual master through initiation.

Manu – Considered the father of the human race and the sovereign of the earth. There are fourteen successive Manus described in the scriptures. The Manusmriti, the code of laws according to Manu, is attributed to Svayambhuva Manu, the earliest of the fourteen Manus. The statement regarding women's protection quoted here is contained in the Manusmriti.

Maya – "Illusion." The Divine Power or veil which conceals Reality and gives the impression of the many, thereby creating the illusion of separation. As maya veils Reality, she deludes us, making us believe that perfection and wholeness are to be found outside of ourselves.

Moksha – Liberation.

Nirguna – Attributeless.

Pada puja – The worship of God's, the guru's or a saint's feet. As the feet support the body, the guru principle supports the Supreme Truth. The guru's feet thus represent the Supreme Truth.

Pandavas – The five brothers, Yudhisthira, Bhishma, Arjuna, Nakula and Sahadeva. They were the sons of King Pandu and the heroes of the epic Mahabharata.

Parabhakti – The highest form of devotion, which is devoid of all desires, in which the devotee experiences his or her oneness with the Beloved Deity who is all-pervasive.

Paramatman – The Supreme Being; Brahman.

Prarabdha – "Responsibilities, burdens." The fruit of past actions from this and past lives, which will manifest in this life.

Puja – Ritualistic or ceremonial worship.

Purana – There are eighteen major Puranas and eighteen minor Puranas. These ancient texts contain stories about the Gods and their incarnations.

Purna – Full, complete, perfect, whole.

Purnavatar – A descent to earth of the nameless, formless, immutable God, assuming a human form. The intention of a divine incarnation is to restore and preserve dharma and to uplift humanity by making it aware of the higher Self.

Rama – "Giver of Joy." The divine hero in the epic, Ramayana. He was an incarnation of Vishnu, and is considered to be the ideal of dharma and virtue.

Rasa-lila – "Ecstatic play." Refers to the dance that took place between Krishna and the gopis in Vrindavan, when He appeared to each of the gopis individually and danced with them all simultaneously.

Ravana – The demon king of Sri Lanka, who is the villain in the Ramayana.

Rishi – Rsi = to know. Self-realized seer; usually refers to the seven rishis of ancient India—Self-realized souls who could "see" the Supreme Truth and expressed this insight through the composition of the Vedas.

Samadhi – Sam = with; adhi = the Lord. Oneness with God; a state of deep, one-pointed concentration, in which all thoughts subside, the mind enters into a state of complete stillness in which only Pure Consciousness remains as one abides in the atman (Self).

Samskara – The totality of impressions imprinted in the mind by experiences from this or earlier lives, which influence the life of a human being—his or her nature, actions, state of mind, etc. It also means the inherent goodness and refinement of character within each person, and the mental disposition and noble qualities one has cultivated in the past.

Sanatana Dharma – "The Eternal Religion," the traditional name for Hinduism.

Sannyasi – A monk or nun who has taken formal vows of renunciation. A sannyasi traditionally wears an ochre-colored cloth, representing the burning away of all body-consciousness.

Satguru – A Self-realized spiritual master.

Satsang – Sat = truth, being; sanga = association with. Being in the company of the wise; also a spiritual discourse by a sage or scholar.

Shakti – Power. Shakti is a name of the Universal Mother, the dynamic aspect of Brahman.

Shiva – "The Auspicious One; the Gracious One; the Good One." A form of the Supreme Being; the masculine

Principle; the static aspect of Brahman. Also, the aspect of the Trinity associated with the destruction of the universe, the destruction of that which is not reality.

Sita – Rama's consort. In India she is considered to be the ideal of womanhood.

Tamas – Darkness; inertia; apathy; ignorance. Tamas is one of the three gunas or fundamental qualities of Nature.

Tapas – "Heat." Self-discipline, austerities, penance and self-sacrifice; spiritual practices which "burn up" the impurities of the mind.

Tapasvi – One engaged in tapas or spiritual austerities.

Tattva – Principle.

Upadhi – A means, medium, or instrument.

Vasana – From "vas" = living, remaining. Vasanas are the latent tendencies or subtle desires within the mind which have a tendency to manifest into action and habits. Vasanas result from the impressions of experiences (samskaras) which exist in the subconscious.

Veda – "Knowledge, Wisdom"; the ancient, sacred scriptures of Hinduism. A collection of holy texts in Sanskrit, which is divided into four parts: Rig, Yajur, Sama and Atharva. They are among the oldest scriptures in the world. The Vedas are considered to be a direct revelation of the Supreme Truth, seen or experienced by the Rishis (realized seers) c:a 5000 B.C.

Vedanta – "Veda-end." The philosophy of the Upanishads, the concluding part of the Vedas, which holds the Ultimate Truth to be "One without a second."

Yoga – "To unite." A series of methods through which one can attain oneness with the Divine; a Path which leads to Self-realization.

Yogi – Someone who is established in the practice of Yoga, or is established in union with the Supreme Being.